ANXIOUS ATTACHMENT RECOVERY GUIDE & WORKBOOK

5 Results-Focused Techniques To Replace Anxious, Needy, Jealous Thoughts With Secure Attachment Behaviors

Copyright © 2024 by LearnWell Books.

All rights reserved. No part of this publication may be reproduced, distributed, or transmitted in any form or by any means, including photocopying, recording, or other electronic or mechanical methods, without the prior written permission of the publisher, except in the case of brief quotations embodied in critical reviews and certain other noncommercial uses permitted by copyright law.

References to historical events, real people, or real places are often fictitious. In such cases, the names, characters, and places are products of the author's imagination. We do this where it's important to protect the privacy of people, places, and things.

689 Burke Rd
Camberwell Victoria 3124
Australia

www.LearnWellBooks.com

We're led by God. Our business is also committed to supporting kids' charities. At the time of printing, we have donated well over $100,000 to enable mentoring services for underprivileged children. By choosing our books, you are helping children who desperately need it. Thank you.

This Is Really Important.
It's a Sincere Thank You.

My name is Wayne, the founder of LearnWell.

My Dad put a book in my hands when I was 13. It was written by Zig Ziglar and it changed the course of my life. Since then, it's been books that have helped me get over breakups, learn how to be a good friend, study the lives of good people and books have been the source of my persistence through some pretty challenging times.

My purpose is now to return the favor. To create books that might be the turning point in the lives of people around the world, just like they've been for me. It's enough to almost bring me to tears to think of you holding this book, seeking information and wisdom from something that I've helped to create. I'm moved in a way that I can't fully explain.

We're a small and 'beyond-enthusiastic' team here at LearnWell. We're writers, editors, researchers, designers, formatters (oh ... and a bookkeeper!) who take your decision to learn with us incredibly seriously. We consider it a privilege to be part of your learning journey. Thank you for allowing us to join you.

If there's anything we did really well, anything we messed up, or anything AT ALL that we could do better, would you please write to us and tell us (like, right now!) We would love to hear from you!

readers@learnwellbooks.com

We're sending you our thanks, our love and our very best wishes.

and the team at LearnWell Books.

WELCOME TO OUR COMMUNITY

"It's like a private online book club"

Imagine if you could actually meet and talk with other readers of this book and share your experiences.

Imagine if you could chat with the author or join them on a live Q&A!

Imagine getting access to the author's notes and other exclusive, unpublished material.

You can do all of that and a lot more in the LearnWell Online Community!!

→ Download your **Workbook**
→ Chat directly with the author!
→ Meet and feel supported by other readers and their experiences.
→ Access additional, exclusive content about this topic and others.
→ Join our live Author Q&A sessions online.
→ Learn faster, make lasting changes, and have 10 times more fun!

This is part of our commitment to creating the best learning resources in the world.

Scan the QR code to get FREE access
www.learnwellbooks.com/securelove

To the anxious heart.

Be calm.
The love you
deserve will
find you.

CONTENTS

Introduction — 10

PART 1: RECOGNIZING AND UNDERSTANDING ANXIOUS ATTACHMENT — 17

1 The Signs, Symptoms, And Impact Of Anxious Attachment — 18
What Makes Our Relationships Hurt So Much

2 The Source Of Your Anxious Attachment — 41
How Upbringing, Life Events, and Personality Shape Your Attachment

PART 2: TRANSFORMING YOUR INNER WORLD — 61

3 Defusing The Triggers — 62
Preventing The Behavioral Explosions

4 How To Remove Negative Thoughts — 76
Making Way For Kindness And Self-Compassion

5 Strong Mind, Strong Relationships — 92
Building Emotional Resilience And Intelligence

PART 3: IMPROVING YOUR RELATIONSHIPS — 101

    6   How To Be Strong — 102
           4 Methods To Restore Your Strength
           In Relationships

    7   Powerful Communicating
        And Clear Boundaries — 115
           How And Where To Draw The Line
           In Your Relationships

    8   Deep Trust, Intimacy, And Vulnerability — 137
           Techniques To Create Closeness

PART 4: STRATEGIES FOR LASTING CHANGE — 159

    9   Secure, In Love, Now, And Forever — 160
           Making Secure Feel Normal

Conclusion — 175

References — 177

YOUR WORKBOOK

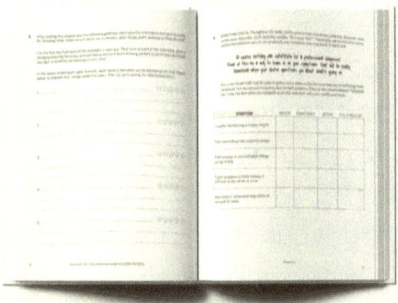

A shocking truth was discovered by a study done in 1987 – **people only remember 10% of what they read!**

That seems so discouraging.

But here's the **GOOD NEWS** – reading is **NEVER** a waste of time. As long as you do **one** important thing ...

The same study (by National Training Laboratories) shows that you will remember 90% of what you read when you **put your new knowledge into action**!

Here at LearnWell, we aim to create **the world's best learning resources**. So, we have included a highly engaging **Workbook** that helps you put your new knowledge into fun, practical action.

So, make sure you download your **FREE Workbook.** You'll find it located inside the **LearnWell Community.** Simply scan the QR code below for access.

Get your Workbook in the LearnWell Community
Scan the QR Code for access or go to:
www.learnwellbooks.com/securelove

INTRODUCTION

Your heart is racing, but you're not moving. You're riveted to your phone, staring at it, willing it to light up with a call, a message, a sign—anything that will quell your frantic need for reassurance.

David told you he would call after work, but it's 8 p.m., and he never finishes after 6. Your mind is spiraling. Is he OK? Has he met someone else? Is he with her now? Is it someone from work? Is that why he's been moody recently?

Your phone buzzes in your hand, startling you. It's David. He's calling. You fumble with the phone as you answer. You inhale sharply as you find your words.

Instead of a calm, warm greeting, all of your tension explodes in a raspy, panicked blast of questions.

"Where are you? Are you OK? I've been so worried. Are you alone?"

David tries to explain that he was caught in a meeting. You barely hear that. You pepper him with more questions, desperately seeking comfort. As the call is finishing, you ask him to come by on his way home. He explains that he's tired and hungry and has an early start. His apparent disinterest throws you into a tailspin of self-doubt.

Your night is ruined. You lay in bed sleepless, replaying every detail of the conversation. You've drafted a lengthy text, punctuated by apologies, professing your love, laced with clinging need, all

Introduction

disguised in a fake kindness. It's 11 p.m. Your finger hovers over the send button as you wrestle with your nervous system, trying to find peace in your uncertainty.

This is anxious attachment.

It's the whirring thoughts, the emotional turbulence, and the perpetual lack of emotional satisfaction, rooted in an insatiable need for validation that remains painfully unforthcoming.

I've been there. I know too well the sleepless nights, the strained relationships, the senseless arguments, and the searing pain in my heart as I drive yet another otherwise promising relationship irretrievably deep into the mud.

I repeated this pattern for years. I dragged several unwitting partners, friends, and other important relationships through my malaise, and I remained largely unconscious of the cycle I was stuck in. As each relationship found its way to its fated end, I concluded that I just wasn't meant to find love. Or at least someone that made me feel worthy of it.

Thankfully, my persistent desire for true love or perhaps my loneliness meant that I wasn't prepared to accept that. I was too young to remain alone, and I knew that true love couldn't elude me forever. So, perhaps just like you now, I went searching for a solution.

Is that where you're at? Have you finally reached the end of a long line of painful experiences that you can no longer blame on 'them'? Have you finally decided to take responsibility for your own happiness rather than just hoping that Mr or Mrs Right will arrive with all of the answers you need?

I hope that this describes where you're at. While I don't wish any of my previous pain on you, I hope you've made a decision to heal and grow, to finally address the cause of your persistent longing.

If that's you, I am so happy you're here. Because I can promise that you will not leave here without all the tools you need to create the safe, secure, nurturing, supportive, caring, respectful relationship you know you deserve.

I have been where you are. I've felt the hurt, the confusion, the self-doubt, and I decided that I would break out of that predictable loop of behaviors

I've spent countless hours in therapy sessions across multiple modalities, from the academic to the wildly experimental. I've read any book of substance on the topic. I've made this the subject of so many conversations, much to the annoyance of family and friends.

But most importantly, I've emerged. I've transcended my own habitual thought patterns and behavioral cycles that kept me from experiencing healthy, loving interactions. I've developed the traits of secure love. I've built thriving relationships, both romantic, platonic, and professional.

I discovered that my anxious attachment wasn't just limited to my love life but my work, my friendships, and even my family. It had become my identity. It was how I interacted with the world.

Introduction

To shift that took some very deep internal work. I have rewritten my view of the world, renewed my values and beliefs, shed the self-doubt that placed a limit on my freedom of expression, and emerged, anew.

With years of this work behind me, I now invite you to benefit from the distilled, refined collection of lessons that have brought me the joy and peace of healthy, secure love.

I have tried, read, and listened to everything I could find, and I've learned what works.

What works are not theories or concepts. What works are those things that cause sustained change.

I'm confident that you've read plenty of material on the topic. I assume you're aware of the basics of attachment theory. If you're anything like me, that information won't help you emerge. It will just validate why you feel the way you do.

That's important, but what's more important is that you make meaningful changes in the way you relate to others. That is the single most important objective of this book – to provoke a sustained, positive change in the way you experience relationships, of all kinds, in your life.

To achieve that, you will discover the 5 simple techniques for managing your thoughts, behaviors, and emotions. You'll learn about the Self-Sabotage Cycle that draws you into a perpetual sequence of destructive patterns. I'll show you how to avoid this as you accumulate the traits of a secure attachment style. In the time that we spend together, you will begin to see these new traits reflected in all your relationships.

I've chosen not to spend time on the theory and background of attachment theory. There are many other great books on those topics. If you need that information, I strongly recommend the following book. It is also published by LearnWell Books and it's arguably the best book available on the topic.

How Attachment Styles Work, LearnWell Books

I didn't bring you a history lesson, and I won't pretend that my advice is a replacement for therapy or the professional diagnosis of mental health conditions.

My advice is very specific. It is designed to help you manage the symptoms of your anxious attachment and practice new methods of thinking, behaving, and feeling that will replace your anxiety with the traits of secure attachment.

The book is structured to deliver a manageable quantity of information in each chapter. You won't be overwhelmed; you'll be refreshed. You'll be able to digest and implement the information at a pace that suits you, and I'm confident that you will feel supported by my deep, authentic interest in your well-being.

I believe we've met here for a reason. I suspect it's because you want healthy love in your life. Perhaps, to date, it's eluded you, but I promise that if you do two things, the love you deserve will not only make its way into your life but will stay with you forever.

What you need to do is:

- Read the book
- Do what I suggest.

To make this easier, and to make sure it happens, I have created an accompanying Workbook that translates all of the suggestions in the book into highly practical exercises and activities. I also understand how important support and validation are for the anxiously attached mind. Let the LearnWell Community be a safe space where you can find the validation and support you need.

I'm honored that you've chosen me to join you on your journey to secure love. You will have to confront some challenging thoughts and emotions, but for all the challenges, the peace and joy you will experience in your relationships will make this journey the most fulfilling of your life.

Thank you in advance for your courage as you pursue life's most precious reward – love.

With my love and support,
Greta

PART 1

RECOGNIZING AND UNDERSTANDING ANXIOUS ATTACHMENT

1

THE SIGNS, SYMPTOMS, AND IMPACT OF ANXIOUS ATTACHMENT

What Makes Our Relationships Hurt So Much

"Anxiety is a thin stream of fear trickling through the mind. If encouraged, it cuts a channel into which all other thoughts are drained."

– Arthur Somers Roche

MY PERSONAL JOURNEY WITH ANXIOUS ATTACHMENT

It started with toast. The burnt kind that can ruin a good morning when you're running out of bread. The kind that had so much potential to be something delicious and warming but which quickly charred when left in for a minute too long. I never thought burnt toast could escalate into a crippling catastrophe. But it did – because I was anxiously attached.

The eggs pattered in the pan as I tried to make conversation. The lack of talking, paired with my partner's softly frowning face as he sipped his coffee, had me feeling edgy. It had been a long week of work for us both; we were notably more tired than usual. I could tell he was looking forward to our breakfast of eggs, toast, and fried tomato to bring some life back into himself.

I know now that his gruff and grumpy demeanor had nothing to do with me, but I didn't know it then. When the toast popped up, dark and inedible, the shift in him opened up a rift of panic in me. My stomach tensed as I scanned his face to find a deepening frown. He let out a sigh and said something about buying bread. I don't know exactly what he said because, in my head, all I heard was, "You never do anything right," and then we argued.

As usual, the argument was senseless and extremely painful. In my mind, I was watching my romantic partner—who I felt was "the one"—slowly slip away from me. My entire existence, sense of self, and safety were tied to the success of this relationship. The argument dropped me so deep into my wounds that it made my reality crumble.

That feeling of losing grip on everything I clung to brought me to my knees and began eroding my dignity. I sobbed and begged for things to be okay again. I wasn't behaving like someone who had gotten into an argument. To me, it was a tragedy. My relationship was dying right before my eyes, and I desperately grappled to save it.

I had gotten into arguments with my partner before. They usually followed a very similar pattern. This pattern played out in many of my relationships, including friendships and at work. Something would go wrong – as things inevitably do in life – and my mind would go into overdrive. My eyes would frantically take in every detail of their face, searching for signs of what I now know was reassurance. My body would begin to surge with anxiety, from a strange tingling in my feet to heat in my face and a blotchy redness across my chest. My thoughts would rapidly descend into a vortex of catastrophizing thoughts like "This is it, he's leaving me," "I knew it, I *am* a burden," and "I can never do enough." I would then begin to fight as if my life depended on it, using any tactic I could to make things better, often only making things much worse.

To varying degrees, my behavior had the potential to put people off, push them away, or cause confusion about my overreactions.

This current argument, where a simple mistake of burnt toast had me questioning my worth, escalated into a conversation with my partner that helped me realize how much of this problem was all me. He was drained and exhausted, pulling further and further away from me each time we argued. And this time, he'd had enough. He grabbed the keys and left.

Hearing the car exit the driveway, my heart sank. I sat in the kitchen alone with the now overcooked eggs. There was nobody to face off with anymore but myself. All my insecurities whirled around my head, spiraling me down into a very dark place – a place that was somehow always there when my partner wasn't around.

Before this moment, every word I spat out was a hand clinging to the back of his shirt. But they weren't kind; they were aggressive and feeble. I began to realize that I had created this situation – the one I fought to avoid.

Before I could change the anxiously attached dynamic I displayed in relationships, I had to spend years figuring out who I really am and why I do the things I do. My healing journey was long and arduous, but eventually, I learned about attachment styles, and I could see myself in every textbook, article, and study I read.

After these years of reflection and active work to heal my wounds, my relationships became safe and loving. With my ever-growing sense of self-worth, my romantic relationship became the safe haven I always sought, but sabotaged. I started being able to get through conflict without putting my dignity on the line. I was no longer the person trying desperately to make my relationships work. They worked without my extraneous coaxing and manipulation. They worked because they relied on the fundamental goodness in both parties and those parties' own health and stability.

Relationships, at the best of times, come with many challenges, but when we heal our anxious attachment, we can prevent those challenges from becoming destructive. To begin to heal, I had to recognize that many of the characteristics of my attachment style would actually be part of my solution. For example, I was so good at analyzing people's behavior, but instead of isolating my focus outward, I now had to turn inward and become acutely aware of my own behavior and the motives behind it.

Anxious attachment comes from deep within us, where all our wounds lie. Although many things can influence attachment styles, they are generally formed during childhood. Our attachment style reflects complex differences in our attachment development, which can lead to an unstable foundation for building self-worth and the myriad cognitive processes upon which healthy relationships are built.

But having an unstable foundation doesn't exclude us from the right to our own healthy, secure relationships. We can apply reinforcements and feel the ground beneath us stabilize. There is much we can do to heal our anxious attachment at its core and move on to find, build, and maintain the relationships we've always dreamed of. We can start by recognizing and understanding why our relationships end up feeling the way they do.

Having an anxious attachment style can feel like there's a veil over us, altering the way we think, feel, and behave. It might feel like we are stuck in a cycle where, no matter what we do, our relationships end up the same. I like to call this cycle of events the Self-Sabotage Cycle Of Anxious Attachment because when we're caught up in it, it can create problems, destroy our relationships, and keep us feeling low. The cycle looks like this:

The Signs, Symptoms, And Impact Of Anxious Attachment

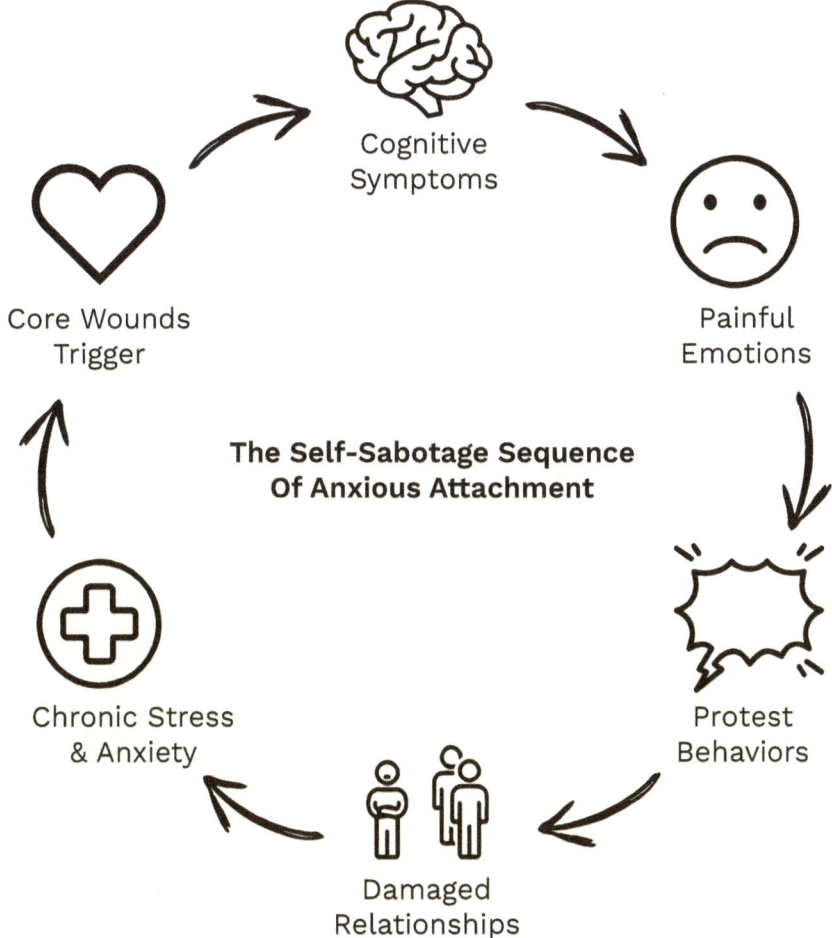

This sequence of events forms a cycle of self-sabotage that perpetuates itself. If we don't find a way to break our patterns, each event throughout the continuous cycle will lead to the next. To begin the healing process, it's important to identify our patterns. Let's explore each part of the Cycle and start to distinguish anxious behavior from healthy behavior in our relationships.

YOUR CORE WOUNDS BECOME TRIGGERED

In the heat of the moment, being anxiously attached can leave us feeling intensely lost, overwhelmed, and confused.[1] We may struggle to pinpoint exactly how we feel, only recognizing a sense of being out of control. Then, once the surge passes, feelings of unworthiness, isolation, and desperation to make things right often linger. Attempts to build a healthy relationship from this low point are often counterintuitive, leading to more dissatisfaction and anxiety.

The dark places that anxious attachment can take us stem from internal wounds. Many, or all, of which we may not be aware of. These wounds are at the core of our struggles and can flare up at the first sign our relationship is in danger. They may also plague our day-to-day lives with insecurities and false beliefs about ourselves or others. We'll break down where these core wounds come from in Chapter 2, but for now, let's take a look at what they are and how they influence the Self-Sabotage Cycle.

Keep in mind that everyone who experiences anxious attachment does so differently. People won't share these 3 core wounds in the same proportions. To understand your own unique version of this attachment style, take a moment now to complete the Workbook activity I've prepared for you. It will increase your awareness of how anxious attachment is impacting your life and relationships.

Wound 1: Constant Worry And Fear Of Abandonment

Anxiously attached people tend to have a deep-seated fear of abandonment.[2] This wound can keep us on edge, constantly watching for signs the other person is pulling away. This watching behavior is also known as being hypervigilant – when you closely monitor the behavior of others, searching for signs of "safety" or "danger." Hypervigilance is a key behavioral trait of anxious attachers, and it's how we are able to pick up on subtle shifts in another person's emotions.[3]

The abandonment wound fuels anxiety because it causes us to perceive distance within relationships as a threat. At its core, it causes fear that people we care about will leave us which may conflate with beliefs that we are a burden, aren't enough, or that we aren't lovable. This can be one of the most difficult wounds to overcome, as it is often reinforced by people inevitably coming and going in our lives for reasons that have little to do with us.

Wound 2: Hypersensitivity To Perceived Rejection Or Criticism

Being rejected is painful for anyone. However, people with an anxious attachment commonly have insecurities about self-worth, which causes hypersensitivity to rejection or criticism.[4] This hypersensitivity often includes perceived rejection or criticism.

The anxiously attached may have strong negative reactions to low-level conflict or constructive criticism. Negative reactions to real or significant moments of rejection or bullying can be considered a normal, sometimes necessary response. But when we suffer a painful response to commonplace interactions with others, this can diminish an already compromised sense of self-worth.

Wound 3: Overwhelming Need For Reassurance And Validation

When we're anxiously attached, we might feel that all we need in a moment of conflict or anxiety is reassurance to make everything okay. Perhaps we feel that we wouldn't lash out or engage in destructive behavior if our partner could simply tell us, loud and clear, that they are committed and happy. The problem is, when we're anxiously attached, reassurance is fleeting.

The wound that makes us hungry for validation and comfort can accompany insecurity within ourselves.[5] We might not have a solid sense of identity, or we may not see ourselves as someone we can fully rely on. Healing this wound and building a sense of security within ourselves takes time and repeated successful moments of self-assurance to recognize our own capability.

Anxious attachment can cause us to focus more on others than we do ourselves, which may cause our inner sense of security to become neglected. We may also experience a tendency to search for security outside ourselves when we feel insecure or upset. This is what can make our attachment style so painful; our relationships have the potential to cause us much pain while simultaneously representing what we may perceive as our safe place or our refuge.

THE COGNITIVE IMPACT

The wounds that lie deep within us can develop into cognitive symptoms like negative thought patterns, false beliefs, or a self-deprecating internal narrative. This part of anxious attachment can suck all the air out of the room for us, and this is what can make our experience feel so mentally heavy. One redeeming feature of the cognitive element in the Self-Sabotage Cycle is that it's where we have the most control. We will explore this further in Part 2.

There are 3 primary cognitive aspects of anxious attachment that perpetuate the mental cycle of insecurity and distress. As you read them below, recognize how much of your own thoughts are "real" and how much are a product of your attachment style. Your Workbook has a helpful exercise to expand on this.

Overanalyzing And Catastrophizing

Disordered thinking is a very common and prominent symptom of any anxiety problem.[6] However, with anxious attachment, disordered thinking patterns will revolve around our relationships. For example, we might spend a lot of time overanalyzing past conversations, emotions, and the behaviors of others or our own behavior in relationships.

Another common disordered thinking pattern is catastrophization. This can involve imagining the worst-case scenarios of future social events, jumping to extreme conclusions about how someone feels or what they're going to do, or having thoughts like "I'm going to be single and alone forever!"

In my case, each time we argued, I'd overanalyze every past negative interaction with my partner and use that information to validate the catastrophizing belief that he'd been secretly planning to leave me all along, and this was the moment I'd been predicting. Disordered thinking patterns feel very real, even if they aren't grounded in reality.

Negative Self-Talk And Self-Blame[7]

Our attachment style can strongly influence our thoughts about ourselves. We might find that we aren't very kind to ourselves and often engage in negative self-talk. This can include an internal narrative that is critical and impatient. We might put ourselves down, hold ourselves to impossibly high standards, and blame ourselves when things go wrong in our relationships, even when those things have nothing or little to do with us.

Difficulty Trusting Oneself And Others

Our lack of inner security breeds distrust for ourselves and others. We may still choose to rely on other people, but that doesn't mean we trust them to fulfill our needs. We might expect them to, but because of the constant cycle of dissatisfaction caused by our attachment style, our feelings of distrust are continuously reinforced.

Trust is a major aspect of secure attachment, which is why there is an entire chapter in Part 3 dedicated to building trust, intimacy, and vulnerability in our relationships.

PAINFUL EMOTIONS THAT WE MAY STRUGGLE TO SELF-SOOTHE

Once our wounds have created destructive cognitive patterns, our thoughts and beliefs can lead to painful emotions. Painful emotions are not necessarily bad, but because an anxious attachment style might be accompanied by difficulties in self-soothing, such emotions can become exacerbated.[8] Here are some common emotions associated with this attachment style.

Intense Fear

One of the most alarming and challenging emotional symptoms of anxious attachment is the intense fear that can come with relationship problems, both perceived and real. This can include feelings of panic when a partner pulls away, constant anxiety or nervousness about our partners' emotions and behavior, and feelings of worry that accompany thoughts about them leaving or rejecting us. Fear can also manifest as desperation, leading to many of the behaviors we will discuss next.

Sadness

Feeling disconnected or neglected by those we love can create strong sadness in our lives. We may lose hope in the idea of finding someone who will love and accept us in the way we crave to be loved. We may not feel as though there is a way out of our self-sabotaging patterns, leading to self-doubt and a feeling that we don't belong with anyone. Anxious attachment can also be a very isolating experience, filled with misunderstandings that can leave us feeling lonely.

Anger

Anxious attachment can cause significant discomfort in our relationships. We may perceive our partners as neglectful or untrustworthy, leading us to thoughts that might trigger fierce anger. In the heat of an argument, our desperation to feel heard and validated might stir up anger if our partners don't respond the way we wish they would.

Anger can also manifest as irritability every time we see our partners enjoying time doing something without us, frustration when they don't pick up the phone when we might think, "Why won't they respond?" or an inner rage that we direct at ourselves when we cause an argument and feel like we've failed again.

Shame

This may follow negative experiences in our relationships that we feel responsible for creating. Our anxious attachment might cause us to exhibit a level of intensity that some people aren't willing to handle. Then, when our intensity is met with negativity or confusion, shame can quickly creep in. We might feel embarrassed about lashing out during an argument or the way we burst into tears about something that "wasn't a big deal."

Thoughts that are associated with shame, such as "I'm too much of a burden on them," can also lead to a sense of unworthiness. We might begin to feel like we aren't good enough or that we are "too flawed" to be in relationships with good people. We might feel as though we are responsible for ruining the relationship, and this can make us feel like we don't deserve our partner's love and affection. These feelings are another reason a person with anxious attachment might not choose secure partners.

Jealousy

I remember when jealousy would strike me deep in the chest each time my partner gave our dog attention. The softness in his voice and the sweet things he would say to her made the emotion surge inside me as I watched our dog receive the attention I deeply craved. It felt silly and embarrassing, but I couldn't help myself. I even went on to build a slight resentment toward our dog for managing to attract my partner's attention when I couldn't.

Jealousy can feel very difficult to navigate because it can trigger many of the other emotions we've just explored. People with anxious attachment might feel a deep sense of shame and guilt for feeling jealous over silly things like a dog getting the attention that they want. We might feel irritated hearing our partners on the phone with family members or lonely and desperate for them to be home with us instead of out having a good time with friends. The type of jealousy that follows anxious attachment can feel unwarranted but difficult to avoid.[9]

PROTEST BEHAVIORS

Reflecting on the complex nature of the negative emotions we've just explored, it's understandable that the behaviors that follow them can be counterintuitive. This is why I refer to this as a 'behavioral dance'. We go back and forth in a push-pull dance with our partners, our emotions, and the actions that follow.

Unfortunately, behaviors driven by strong, painful emotions are capable of tremendous damage in relationships. These kinds of behaviors, also known as protest behaviors, form part of the behavioral dance, creating scenarios that may provoke our greatest fears. Protest behaviors are the destructive things we do with the intention of drawing our partners closer.[10] They are what give the other person in our relationships fuel to behave in counterintuitive ways. These protest behaviors can include, amongst others:

- Clinginess and excessive attempts to please.
- Neglecting our own boundaries and needs.
- Testing and other manipulation tactics.

Protest behaviors are what we may automatically implement as a knee-jerk reaction to the way that we feel. If our emotions are causing feelings of desperation, panic, or anger, they may feel so intense and overwhelming that we naturally do what we think will help us find relief – which is likely seeking reassurance, comfort, or validation from our partners because we may not feel able to self-soothe sufficiently.

These behaviors can attract partners or friends with insecure attachment styles, particularly those with avoidant attachments, as they make the perfect match for the push-and-pull behavioral dance.[11] As you prepare for the Workbook exercise at the end of this chapter, see if you can identify these behaviors in your relationships and consider how your wounds and emotions might lead you to them.

Clinginess And Excessive Attempts To Please Others

Anxious attachers are often very outward-focused, hyper-analyzing the behaviors and emotions of others in an attempt to avoid abandonment. This can appear as clinginess, where we might try to check in with our partners too often, ask them how they're feeling constantly, or experience extreme anxiety when a bid for connection isn't reciprocated straight away.

It can also present as people-pleasing behaviors such as doing things for others even when our own cup is completely empty, taking responsibility to soothe others' negative emotions, walking on eggshells to avoid conflict, and being overly agreeable, contrary to our own feelings and desires. In the worst-case scenario, we might find ourselves crossing our partner's boundaries by constantly surprising them at work or messaging their family to gain reassurance about the relationship.

Neglecting Our Own Boundaries And Needs

If we have low self-worth, it becomes difficult to recognize our own needs and boundaries. We might brush them aside to please others, or we might completely forget that our needs and boundaries matter.[12] We matter, but anxious attachment can make us forget that.

Anxious attachers are often not very good at communicating our needs clearly and concisely. We might hear ourselves rambling on in an attempt to fix a situation or express how we feel. Our emotions might turn what we intended to say into a mess of overexplaining, complaining, or emotional intensity. This is such a common challenge for anxious attachers that there's an entire chapter on communication and setting boundaries in Part 3.

The Push-Pull Dynamic In Action

The idea of anxious attachment might paint the image of someone who is excessively clingy, needy, or vulnerable all the time. But the push-pull dynamic has two sides to it. It can also appear in the form of a self-protective mechanism to avoid being abandoned, where we might exhibit certain behaviors natural to our attachment style (pulling behaviors) and then suddenly switch to protective behaviors in an attempt to appear more secure (pushing behaviors). Some examples of the push-pull dynamic include:

- Seeking reassurance (pull) and then soon after the security of that reassurance fades, withdrawing emotionally out of a fear that it won't last, wasn't true, or was too much to ask (push).

- Demanding attention in a way that leads to conflict (pull) and then rejecting attention and contact out of fear that our neediness is driving our partners away (push). This could also be accompanied by fleeting negative thoughts like "I'm better alone anyway."

- Being overly attentive to our partner's needs (pull) and then abruptly detaching to avoid coming across as too clingy (push), accidentally leaving our partners emotionally high and dry.

The push-pull dynamic may also be used to manipulate our partners into giving us the attention and reassurance we crave. For example, we might give the silent treatment or threaten to leave, hoping that these behaviors will cause our partners the same anxiety we would likely feel in those scenarios so that they draw closer.

Testing And Other Manipulation Tactics

Many protest behaviors can verge on being emotionally abusive. Much like the push-pull dynamic, our anxious attachment can mean that we use other manipulation tactics to try and draw our partners closer. These tactics can be a more circuitous path to get the attention or reassurance we seek.

'Testing' is a manipulation tactic in which we intentionally create a scenario that challenges our relationship's strength. For example, we might pack our bags after an argument with our partners, hoping that they will panic and beg us to stay—proving that they care. Other tactics might include making our partners jealous by flirting with other people and telling lies or making up stories to get comfort, reassurance, or physical closeness.

THE DAMAGE TO RELATIONSHIPS

On the journey ahead, you will find comfort in the myriad ways I'll share to create security in yourself, your relationship, and your life. But first, let's uncover the impact that anxious attachment has on relationships.

Not just romantic relationships. All of them.

Anxious attachment is full of destructive patterns that can influence every area of life, including work, family time, and leisure activities. It can show up in our approach to parenting, leadership, teaching skills, or even the way we interact with strangers.

Before we continue, I want to acknowledge that anxious attachment is not all bad. There are many ways that our sensitivity and empathy towards others can make our relationships great. However, when the wounds, protest behaviors, and cognitive symptoms are left unresolved, anxious attachment can significantly strain our relationships. It can quickly and often unconsciously drive us into self-sabotaging behavior.

Strained Romantic Relationships

Anxious attachment wounds are most commonly known for flaring up in romantic relationships. They can include any combination of all the thought patterns, emotions, and behaviors we've discussed. However, these experiences may not always remain isolated to challenging times or occasional arguments. They can lead to relationships that are unhealthy overall and destructive for both parties.[13]

Left unchecked, our attachment style can lead us to create romantic relationships filled with painful and frequent arguing, emotional games that sever connections, and even manipulation, controlling behavior, and emotional abuse. It's an ugly but unfortunately common outcome of ignoring attachment wounds in romantic relationships.[14]

Challenges In Friendships And Social Interactions

In friendships and other social interactions our anxious attachment might show up in the form of neediness, jealousy when our friends spend time with other friends, or getting into arguments easily. We might perceive rejection when our friends don't text us back soon enough, worry that they secretly don't like us, or we might find ourselves playing emotional games with them to test whether they really care about us.

Anxious attachment might also cause us to attract friends who genuinely aren't supportive or who take advantage of our kind and caring nature. If our attachment style happens to be isolated to our romantic relationships, our obsession with our relationships and our partner could then cause us to neglect our friendships as we detach ourselves from them while our relationships consume our identities.

Difficulties In Work And Professional Settings

When we deal with symptoms of anxious attachment for a long time, our sense of identity, self-worth, and confidence are impacted. In a professional environment, confidence and a strong sense of self are necessary traits for success. If we constantly self-abandon because of our attachment wounds, find that our minds are distracted by over-analyzing and catastrophizing, or face problems at work with excessive anxiety and emotional instability, our careers can suffer, too. Anxious attachment can reach every area of our lives.

Family Dysfunction And Parenting Problems

If we have children, our own unhealed attachment wounds can influence the security of our children's attachment style.[15] This can happen because our wounds influence our parenting or because of the volatile relationships we may have with our partners. Anxious attachment can make home life feel unsafe or inconsistent and have a significant impact on our families.

CHRONIC STRESS, ANXIETY AND THE IMPACT ON OUR BODIES

When we're caught up in the Self-Sabotage Cycle, stress and anxiety can become chronic, leading to serious health consequences.[16] When we don't feel well physically, it is much more difficult to restore ourselves emotionally to then find the strength to heal our wounds. Poor health can exacerbate mental health struggles like depression and anxiety, ultimately making our core wounds more difficult to heal.[17]

Chronic Stress And Its Health Consequences

When we experience stress, our bodies enter a complex cycle of internal processes designed to combat the stress and help us recover. However, when stress becomes chronic, this cycle can't be completed, and our bodies are negatively impacted. Chronic stress can compromise our immune systems, disrupt hormones, and damage organs, leading to disease.[18]

Sleep Disturbances And Fatigue

As many as one-third of adults experience sleep disturbances, and anxiety is considered one of the most common psychological causes, including attachment anxiety.[19] It can cause or contribute to insomnia, wake us up from a peaceful sleep, or influence the general quality of our sleep.

Chronic stress and anxiety cause sleep issues because they activate our fight-or-flight nervous system response – which puts us on edge and prepares us for danger. They cause our bodies to create more of the stress hormone known as cortisol, which can interfere with sleep. However, once our sleep is negatively impacted by stress, our cortisol levels continue to rise, and the cycle perpetuates.[20]

Sleep problems will make us wake up feeling unrested and contribute to fatigue that lasts all day. Fatigue can cause brain fog, irritability, and a type of anxiety that may be described as "tired but wired."[21]

Muscle Tension And Pain

The chronic anxiety that often comes with anxious attachment can cause muscle tension, inflammation, and discomfort in our bodies. This is because the musculoskeletal system of the body is strongly impacted.

When stress becomes chronic, muscles can enter a state of constant tension that promotes the formation of long-term problems like chronic pain and headaches. This impact on the musculoskeletal system is one of the leading causes of tension headaches or migraines.[22]

THE JOURNEY AHEAD

Being anxiously attached can trap us in the Self-Sabotage Cycle where we repeat the same patterns of feelings, thoughts, and behaviors. Often in devastating ways. This is not just a relationship issue. It's a holistic life issue.

That's why, throughout this book, I share a variety of techniques that will help you break free from this Cycle so you can experience the security in relationships and life that you deserve.

In the next chapter, you'll learn how your attachment style was formed so you can understand the wounds responsible for many of the challenging thoughts, emotions, and behaviors you may exhibit. But before you do, take a moment with your Workbook. It contains an exercise where you create your attachment profile—a blueprint of how your attachment style impacts you.

2

THE SOURCE OF YOUR ANXIOUS ATTACHMENT

How Upbringing, Life Events, and Personality Shape Your Attachment

"Our stresses, anxieties, pains and problems arise because we do not see the world, others or even ourselves as worthy of love."

– *Prem Prakash*

THIS IS YOUR ATTACHMENT HISTORY

If you were to peek through my childhood bedroom after 7 pm, you'd see the perfect picture of a mother lovingly tucking her daughter into bed. She'd be reading bedtime stories before kissing goodnight and making sure to leave a crack in the door to let a little light in from the hall. However, what you wouldn't see was the physical lashing out after a minor inconvenience that happened just hours before. You wouldn't see the confusion on my young face as I scanned my mom's expression to find rage breaking through a forced smile. You wouldn't see the tip-toeing, eggshell-walking fear that was already so prominent in my childhood.

If you were to continue watching, like a fly on the wall, you would also not foresee that the goodnight kiss you witnessed was actually goodbye. You'd see that same loving mother packing her bags and abandoning her children to leave them behind with their father – a father who now needed to work, cook, clean, run errands, and raise two daughters on his own.

Attachment styles form in early childhood in response to our primary caregivers. After about 6 months of age, we become able to anticipate how our caregivers will respond to our needs, especially during times of distress, and we begin to shape our own behaviors accordingly. [23]

A secure attachment results from having caregivers who are consistently loving and sensitive to our needs, particularly during times of distress. However, much like in my attachment history, anxious attachment develops when caregivers are inconsistent with their love and sensitivity.[24] They may respond to our distress in confusing or unexpected ways, or they may show up to support us one moment and then become overwhelmed or distant the next.

Parenting that may lead to anxious attachment might include parents who:

- Lose their temper or experience sudden mood changes.
- Become critical of their children or withhold affection when their child doesn't meet their standards.
- Display inconsistent conflict resolution skills, perhaps resorting to shouting or hitting.
- Withdraw emotionally as a form of punishment or lack of emotional regulation.
- Restrict their child's independence by being overly involved or overprotective.

This attachment style can also form when caregivers suffer from chronic illness.[25] Any situation that might cause a caregiver to display inconsistent parenting or instill fear and anxiety in a child could lead to the development of anxious attachment.

Reflecting on my attachment history helped me understand why I naturally responded to my relationships the way that I did. I felt excessively dependent on them for my internal sense of security, even when they didn't meet my expectations. I was hypervigilant about their emotions and behaviors, constantly searching for signs that they were unhappy. I didn't feel confident tackling problems alone, or at least not without external validation. I didn't trust myself to make the "right" choices or do the "right" things. But it all made sense once I looked back.

Many of these were patterns I had developed from constantly having to analyze my mom's behavior for signs of distress or withdrawal. They also became exacerbated after she left suddenly because of the profound abandonment wound I developed.

As painful as it was looking so closely at some of the most difficult times of my childhood, it was a necessary part of my healing journey. In this chapter, I will encourage you to do the same. We will discuss the harmful parenting styles, adverse life events, and innate personality traits that may influence anxious attachment. Give each section careful thought. Revelations may occur to you about about how your own anxious attachment was formed.

At the end of this chapter, there will be a Workbook activity to guide your through creating your own attachment history. Understanding your wounds will also be important in Part 2.

The only caveat is that you move forward without judgment. Looking at the source of our attachment wounds is not about blaming our caregivers for their mistakes or circumstances. It's important that we stay objective during this process and simply consider how we developed an anxious attachment to better understand ourselves and show ourselves compassion.

EARLY CHILDHOOD EXPERIENCES AND ATTACHMENT FORMATION

Our early childhood experiences, starting at around 6 months old, contribute to the development of our attachment style because this is when we first learn that we are separate from our primary caregivers.[26] From birth we have an innate ability to attract our caregiver's attention, crying when we have a need such as hunger, hygiene, or physical closeness. However, from 6 months onward, we may begin to change our behavior to ensure we get our needs met.

If our caregivers have inconsistent parenting styles, we may use our behavior to mitigate their inconsistency. An anxious child might cling to their parent in unfamiliar environments. They may fear new people, go quiet around them, or resist attempts to connect. They may experience extreme distress when separated from their caregiver, which could include excessive crying, emotional overwhelm, and even panic attacks.[27]

There are many parenting styles that may lead to attachment anxiety in children.[28] Here are a few archetypes based on those parenting styles that could lead to anxious attachment, keeping in mind that they are not definitive. Our parents may fit several or none of them:

The "Disciplinarian"

This parent can be very caring when their short fuse isn't getting triggered. However, they may be prone to overreacting to minor inconveniences and using extreme disciplinary measures such as hitting, shouting, or other fear-based tactics.

Beyond being a parent, this archetype may be a perfectionist. However, that causes them to have unrealistically high standards, and they constantly monitor their children for mistakes and flaws. They may also be highly critical.

Even though this parent may exhibit a lot of great qualities when things are okay, their harsh disciplinarian behaviors lead to broken parent-child connections. They can break trust each time it is rebuilt and lead to children with a negative internal narrative. The anxiety that comes when a child experiences this kind of parenting style may include false beliefs that they deserve such treatment or that they are flawed.

When we experience a parenting style like this, there are several emotional needs that may go unmet. They can include:

- Feelings of safety around our caregiver.

- Unconditional love needed for secure development.

- Autonomy and the freedom to make healthy mistakes.

- Fair and appropriate discipline to teach boundaries.

- Open and healthy communication.

- Encouragement and guidance.

Remember, having insecure attachment doesn't mean our caregivers were bad people or didn't love us. It's still possible for good people to hurt the ones they love. Parents with harmful parenting styles are often fighting their own internal battles or dealing with overwhelming circumstances. What's important is that we can simultaneously recognize the harm in how we may have been parented while showing our parents a degree of compassion.

Your Workbook includes an exercise for you to make a list of the parenting styles you experienced growing up. You don't have to pick one of the archetypes below; you can include points and behaviors from each to complete your picture. As you continue, revisit the Workbook exercise to add more points that resonate with your experience. This list will form part of your attachment history.

The Overprotector

As well-meaning as this parent may be, their overprotective behavior can potentially encourage anxious attachment in a number of ways. This parent may instill fears in their children about the world and its many potential dangers, either knowingly or unknowingly. They may become over-involved in their children's activities, often stepping in to "help" their children overcome normal developmental challenges.

The overprotective parent's high anxiety might cause them to restrict their child from enjoying normal childhood activities like going on school field trips or having sleepovers with friends. They may also live in fear that they aren't doing enough for their child, causing a tendency to overcompensate in unhelpful ways.

While this parenting style may include many good qualities, like intense care and love, the anxiety that drives overprotective behavior may unintentionally transfer to the children involved. This style may create children who are scared to try new things or who don't feel safe doing things alone. They may be overly clingy or require a lot of reassurance from their caregivers.

When we experience a parenting style like this, the emotional needs that may go unmet can include:

- Opportunities for social development.

- Freedom to take risks and learn risk assessment and coping skills.

- A sense of autonomy and interdependence.

- Encouragement to face challenges and build resilience.

- Space to develop emotional regulation skills.

We may look back on a childhood filled with nurturing and love and wonder why we developed an insecure attachment style. In this scenario, our caregivers may have had good intentions to keep us safe from negative experiences but inadvertently blocked us from developing an inner sense of security or experiencing healthy childhood struggles necessary for proper social and emotional development.

The Hot-And-Cold Parent

The crux of this parenting style is emotional inconsistency. Sometimes, they offer warmth and comfort, and other times, they withdraw or explode for reasons that may be unclear to the child. The hot-and-cold parent might explode with anger when something goes wrong and then quickly pull away without resolving the problem. They may struggle to regulate their own emotions or offer adequate comfort when their child is distressed.

The hot-and-cold parent can still be a loving parent who is plagued with guilt about their behavior. They may overcompensate for their behavior by buying gifts, spending money or time on gestures and activities, or suddenly becoming overly attentive.

A child growing up with a hot-and-cold caregiver may develop anxious attachment as they become hypervigilant about their caregivers' behavior. They may cling to their caregiver when they are receiving comfort and warmth while staying on high alert for signs that their caregiver is going to explode or pull away. Experiencing emotional inconsistency can impact a child's self-worth as they might grow to believe that they are deserving of their parent's emotional withdrawal or volatility.

This parenting style can leave certain emotional needs unmet in childhood, including:

- Feelings of safety and security around their primary caregiver.

- Emotional validation and repair after conflict or distress.

- Clarity around boundaries and expectations, especially after conflict.

- Unconditional emotional support and comfort.

- A sense of trust and predictability between caregiver and child.

This childhood experience may have created an unstable home environment and a dysfunctional family dynamic. It may have felt confusing and unpredictable, leaving the child on high alert for the next incident. Once the incident subsided, the child may have been left to ascertain the cause, potentially coming to false conclusions or taking responsibility.

The Emotional Manipulator

This parenting style might include many moments when a parent appears loving and sensitive only to have a more self-serving motive. Or, there may be times when this parent is genuinely loving and supportive, but because they may use emotional manipulation often, their children may not trust or be able to properly decipher their caregiver's motives.

A parent with this style may use manipulation tactics to punish their children or win back their affection. They may say things during an argument to gain validation, like "You think I'm the worst Mother" or "I've sacrificed so much for you, and this is the thanks I get." This parent may use silent treatment or purposefully neglect their child's needs as a form of punishment. They may also deny their child's experience of a scenario in order to remain in control or in high regard.

Beneath the surface, this parent is self-centered and feels anxious about how others perceive them. They may feel a strong desire to be liked by everyone and lack the emotional intelligence to handle conflict maturely. They may strongly wish to be viewed as a great parent rather than actively working to be one, using their tactics to govern the perceptions of others.

Their children might struggle to trust their own judgment, experiencing intense anxiety and confusion when their experiences are denied. They may lack confidence in their problem-solving abilities and believe that they aren't capable of making good decisions without the input of others. These children might also learn, by their parents' example, to use manipulation or emotional suppression to get attention and validation if they fail to achieve this through authentic behavior.

As one of the most damaging parenting styles, the emotionally manipulative parent may neglect the following needs:

- A healthy model of honesty and integrity.
- Emotional safety and security through consistent care.
- A secure sense of self, fostered by consistent and honest feedback.
- Acknowledgment and validation of experiences.
- Healthy and consistent conflict resolution.
- Genuine affection and support.

This parenting style involves behavior that would be classified as emotional abuse. However, even a well-meaning parent may resort to emotional manipulation if they don't have a secure sense of self or perhaps struggle with mental illness. The early childhood experiences that may come with having a manipulative primary caregiver could also exceed regular insecure attachment and contribute to other effects of trauma, including PTSD.[29]

The Effects Of Trauma On The Developing Brain And Attachment System

Trauma is an important topic to understand on our healing journey as it is the main contributor to insecure attachment in one form or another. This is because the unmet needs that cause insecure attachment in childhood constitute trauma.[30]

Trauma of any kind can have a significant impact on the developing brain and attachment system of a person because it activates the body's biological stress response. When this stress response is activated at a chronic level, the developing brain and nervous system can become maladapted. This can lead to long-term physiological and psychological risks such as chronic illness, including autoimmune issues, and mental illnesses like depression and anxiety disorders.[31]

However, trauma does not necessarily need to happen within a specific window of development to impact attachment style. Attachment styles formed in childhood can change after more recent trauma or adverse life events.

TRAUMA AND ADVERSE LIFE EVENTS

While the parenting styles we've discussed can lead to a childhood experience of trauma, primary caregivers are not always responsible for a person's attachment style. Even a person who develops secure attachment in childhood can exhibit insecure attachment after exposure to trauma or an adverse life event.[32]

As we explore how trauma influences attachment, gently consider if trauma may form part of your attachment history. There is space in the Workbook activity of this chapter for you to include any life events or trauma that may have happened later in your life to influence the outcome of your attachment style.

The Relationship Between Trauma And Anxious Attachment

The relationship between trauma and anxious attachment is multifaceted and complex. Trauma itself is a complex subject with a wide spectrum of experiences that may or may not be classified as trauma. What's important to understand is that trauma is classified on an individual basis – an experience may be traumatic to one and not to others.

In psychology, trauma can be separated into what is commonly referred to as "big T trauma" and "little t trauma".[33] Big T traumas are the obvious traumatic events that are easy to recognize. In relationship to anxious attachment, these can include the sudden loss of a parent, severe adverse interactions with caregivers or family members, having a caregiver with mental illness, or other big traumatic events and experiences. Little t traumas that can contribute to anxious attachment include moments where needs went unmet, like all the unmet needs we discussed as part of the parenting archetypes above.[34]

Trauma does not need to be severe or sudden to impact your attachment style. Unmet needs in childhood can constitute as little t trauma and are enough to form insecure attachment. However, trauma later in life can also impact attachment style. It's possible for attachment styles to shift, improve, or worsen following a catalyst like trauma, too.[35]

Types Of Trauma That Can Influence Attachment Style

Attachment styles can change as a result of trauma, just as they can change in response to personal growth and development.[36]

For trauma to influence attachment style, it will generally need to happen in relation to important relationships like friendships or romantic relationships.[37] Much like how caregivers influence attachment styles in childhood, our relationship experiences in adulthood can greatly influence changes in attachment. The types of trauma that can change or influence attachment styles later in life can fall within two categories: big-t relationship trauma and little-t relationship trauma.

Big T Relationship Trauma

This may include any major or sudden adverse life events that impact your relationship, such as:

- Losing a romantic partner who passed away suddenly.
- Severe illness or disability within a relationship.
- Betrayal or a suddenly severed connection, eg. infidelity.
- A shared life-threatening experience with a partner.
- Physical violence or assault within a relationship.
- Sudden financial crisis like bankruptcy or falling victim to a scam.

Little T Relationship Trauma

A relationship doesn't have to include any big T trauma to influence our attachment styles. Simply being in a relationship with someone who is insecurely attached, neglectful, emotionally abusive, or constantly dysregulated can slowly shift our attachment behavior in response.[38]

For example, someone who is securely attached might become anxiously attached in a relationship with someone exhibiting avoidant attachment traits. If someone we love constantly pulls away from us, it doesn't take insecure attachment to experience anxiety as a response. Similarly, If someone with anxious attachment constantly perceives rejection within a relationship and reacts by clinging and reaching out to their partners too often for reassurance, this can cause a secure partner to pull away, exhibiting avoidant behavior.

It's also possible for someone with insecure attachment to become more secure in a particular relationship if the parameters of the relationship naturally soothe or fulfill our attachment needs.[39]

Little t trauma in relationships that may influence attachment style in adulthood includes any combination of minor or longer-lasting trauma, such as:

- Having partners who criticize us, say things that undermine our character, or who may even bully us into doing things we don't want to do. For example, having a partner who pressures you into drinking, calls you names, or makes hurtful comments about you.

- Experiencing emotional abuse or neglect within a relationship where our partners might use manipulation tactics to get their needs met or to deny our needs. For example, a partner who won't take responsibility for bad behavior and who walks out during arguments without trying to resolve the conflict later. They may also emotionally withdraw, giving the silent treatment until we apologize – even though we weren't solely responsible for the conflict.

- Watching our partners engage in "minor" infidelity issues such as flirting or texting other people in inappropriate ways. They may also deny that there is anything wrong with their behavior or justify their behavior to make us feel like we're being too restrictive.

- Feeling like our partners are inconsistent in their availability or unpredictabe with their love and affection. For example, a partner who goes out of their way to express their love through a romantic gesture, only to pull back again for some time after. This relationship might feel like it's going nowhere because our partner's words and actions don't align.

- Having a partner who uses passive-aggressive behavior to communicate their emotions and needs. For example, noisily completing a household task to communicate their frustration with us leaving that task incomplete rather than openly communicating their feelings.

- Invalidation of achievements or experiences, where a partner may undermine the value of our achievements or deny the validity of our experiences within or outside the relationship. For example, scoffing at our enthusiasm after running a marathon or saying something like "Let me tell you what *really* happened" after we've expressed our truth about a situation.

- Crossing boundaries that we have made clear. For example, having a partner who switches their phone off and stays out past midnight despite our sincere boundaries about communication and reasonable time out with friends. This can also include having a partner who consistently pushes against our basic boundaries like personal space, private items, and financial limits. For example, having a partner who continues to spend past the limit on the household credit card, or who invades our privacy by searching our drawers or reading our texts.

So much about our circumstances, relationships, and childhood experiences can shape the way we think, feel, and behave. These are all aspects of our external environment that can influence our attachment styles. However, it's possible to have innate qualities that may make us more susceptible to internalizing trauma and forming insecure attachment.[40]

TEMPERAMENT AND ATTACHMENT STYLE

If we have innate qualities that make us more susceptible to forming an anxious attachment, it doesn't mean that the trauma we experience isn't valid, only that we may have a more sensitive or anxious constitution to begin with. That may make the small t traumas we experience more impactful on our development.[41]

We can also exhibit behavioral traits associated with a different attachment style due to our natural temperament. For example, if we are naturally sensitive people, we may already be prone to experiencing anxiety in life, independent of our attachment style. Additionally, a person with an innate proclivity towards anxiety can still develop secure or avoidant attachment.

However, in combination with complimentary childhood experiences, innate anxious qualities may leave us more susceptible to developing anxious attachment. Such qualities can include:

- Natural sensitivity to environmental stimuli.[42] This could make having a parent who shouts or who has higher physical energy more impactful.

- Heightened physiological response to stress.[43] This could cause normal stressors or trauma to feel more intense and to be harmful.

- Inherent difficulties regulating emotions or experiencing emotions more intensely.[44] This can cause stressors to quickly become overwhelming and contribute to anxiety.

- Genetic predisposition to anxiety. It's possible to have a genetic predisposition to anxiety, where a person has a family history of anxiety or other mood disorders, leaving them neurologically more prone to anxiety.[45]

Although it may feel frustrating to have innately anxious qualities, it doesn't mean the hope of building a more secure attachment is lost. Consider your innate temperament and how it might influence your attachment style. This will form part of your attachment history. Add any innate traits you may associate with your attachment style to your Workbook exercise.

MOVING FORWARD

It's important to recognize that your unique attachment history is one that has led you to this moment and contributed to many of your experiences. But you get to choose if it continues to be a part of your story. How you currently behave in relationships is, for the most part, learned behavior. It does not define your future behavior. You can build a future of security in yourself and around others.

As we continue to Part 2, we will begin working on the necessary steps and techniques to exit the Self-Sabotage Cycle – starting with the triggers that give our wounds life.

Take a moment now to visit your Workbook and complete your attachment history. You can refer back to it when you feel unsure of your anxious behaviors and thoughts as a reminder that what you experience is understandable, considering what you've been through. You might like to share about it on the LearnWell Community too. Once you're done, know that there is so much to look forward to from here onwards.

PART 2

TRANSFORMING YOUR INNER WORLD

3

DEFUSING THE TRIGGERS

Preventing The Behavioral Explosions

"Attachment principles teach us that most people are only as needy as their unmet needs"

– Amir Levine

THE DEVASTATING ROLE OF TRIGGERS IN ANXIOUS ATTACHMENT

The moment I saw my partner's frown deepen at the burnt toast, it was as if a part of me time-traveled back to childhood. That part within me – my inner child – was seeing my mom's face change in response to a mess I'd made or a mistake I'd tried to hide. That small but vulnerable inner child was feeling the fear of what came next all over again. She anticipated the explosive anger, the unexpected lashing out, and the abandonment. Like a moment in time playing on a loop, this hidden trauma was resurfacing every time something in my relationship triggered those wounds.

The wounds we sustained during childhood, adolescence, and adulthood that may have impacted our attachment styles don't necessarily influence our thoughts, feelings, and behaviors unless something – a trigger – causes them to surface. However, when we are anxiously attached, it can feel like these wounds are ever present because of the prevalence of triggers within relationships. For some of us, just being in a romantic relationship can be a trigger on its own. Once someone good comes into our lives, the abandonment wound can become activated, and we may constantly fear losing what we have.[46]

As seen in the Self-Sabotage Cycle that we explored in Chapter 1, a wound that becomes triggered can quickly progress into thoughts and emotions that amplify the experience. Then, once the intensity of our feelings is heightened, our behavior can appear exaggerated in relation to the problem we're facing. We may become defensive even when the person in front of us is not directing any blame toward us. We may begin to shout or sharpen our tone of voice as we become overwhelmed by a minor conflict.

We may jump to conclusions about our partner's experience, forgetting all the positive reinforcement they've given us in the past. We may not feel able to listen clearly. And, often, we may not understand our own reactions.

The emotional blowups, anxiety, and other amplified negative experiences we encounter in relationships can feel spontaneous. But if we look carefully, there is almost always a trigger that precedes our thoughts, feelings, and behaviors in these situations. Learning to recognize our triggers and understand them will give us more control over what comes next.

When we manage triggered wounds effectively, we can reduce the intensity of The Self-Sabotage Cycle or even break out of it entirely. Triggers are opportunities for us to know ourselves better and gently heal.

Throughout this chapter, I'll show you how to identify your triggers and mindfully move through them using a trigger response technique known as EGO. I'll also give you examples of common triggers for anxiously attached people and some steps you can take to personalize the EGO trigger response technique.

IDENTIFYING AND UNDERSTANDING OUR TRIGGERS

Almost any event, or combination of events, can constitute a trigger. A trigger can include something somebody says to us, a certain type of environment, or even things like smell, taste, and sound.[47]

There was a time when my partner having a drink with friends would cause a significant rift between us. I would become filled with anxiety and constantly check in with him. Then, if he would come to bed with even a hint of alcohol on his breath, I'd completely withdraw and spend the next few days avoiding him and using passive-aggressive behavior in the hopes he would apologize – for having 2 drinks at a family restaurant.

In my example, the combination of my partner drinking alcohol and any indication of altered behavior triggered me because it reminded me of a previous partner who struggled with addiction. Some part of me would fear two very painful things: Firstly, that my partner would slowly develop an addiction if he continued to enjoy alcohol, and secondly, that he would end up treating me the same way my previous partner did.

To make it clear, my triggers in this scenario included a combination of things:

- My partner leaving the house to drink with friends.
- Any altered behavior as a result of drugs or alcohol.
- The smell of alcohol on my partner's breath.

Looking back on this, my triggers made a lot of sense. But because I wasn't aware of them, I unintentionally held my current partner to unfair standards, even though he never gave me any reason to expect the same outcome in our relationship as a result of his occasional drinking.

When a trigger occurs, it's not always obvious what it is. We may become "triggered," suddenly experiencing strong cognitive, emotional, and physiological symptoms without understanding what set us off.

As you continue to read, consider whether some of the following examples fit with your story. It can be far easier to recognize a trigger in hindsight than in the heat of the moment. Becoming familiar with your triggers will help you become more accustomed to catching yourself when being triggered and recognizing what behaviors, words, or events got you there.

How To Know When We're Triggered

The first step to understanding your triggers is identifying when you are in a triggered emotional state. Recognizing when you are becoming triggered will significantly improve your ability to notice what came before. So, let's look at some of the common symptoms. They can include both psychological and physiological experiences, as shown below:

Psychological Symptoms Of Triggered Anxious Attachment[48]

- Intense worry about the relationship or our partner's behavior.

- Overwhelming fear of abandonment, rejection, or infidelity.

- Hypervigilance to behaviors, facial expressions, and any other signs of a negative outcome.

- A sudden strong urge to be close and feel connected to our partners.

- Mood swings, such as a sudden switch from sadness to anger.

- A negative internal narrative and low self-esteem with thoughts about being unlovable or not good enough.

- Emotional outbursts with shouting, crying, or sudden withdrawal in an attempt to feel heard and understood.

- Obsessively thinking about when our partners will be home or their relationship with people we perceive as threatening.

- Persistent feelings of jealousy that can feel out of place or intense suspicion that can feel valid even when there is no evidence to support it.

- Desperation for reassurance or comfort from our partners, especially after we've pushed them away with our words or behaviors.

Physiological Symptoms Of Triggered Anxious Attachment[49]

These symptoms are important to pay attention to, as they may precede more obvious psychological signs. Our bodies can be the first to tell us when our wounds have been triggered because trauma changes our bodies' physiological stress response.[50] That can mean our bodies are able to pick up on stressors and respond to them physiologically before we've even realized we're triggered.

As you look out for these signs of physiological arousal in response to a trigger, try to notice what happened almost immediately before:

- Feeling our heart rates quicken, a pounding sensation in the chest, or experiencing palpitations.

- Starting to sweat excessively or suddenly becoming hot under our clothing. We may also feel our faces warm and see our cheeks redden if we look in a mirror.

- Becoming short of breath, hyperventilating, or having difficulty breathing that has no other obvious cause.

- Trembling or shaking throughout our bodies that feels like intense shivering without another obvious cause.

- Feeling our stomachs tensing, experiencing nausea, or feeling butterflies in our stomachs. Sometimes, just words or actions can even make us feel like we've been punched in the stomach.

- Experiencing a tension headache or migraine coming on soon after a negative relationship event.

There are also some physiological responses to being triggered that can be longer lasting, such as:

- Tense and sore muscles, especially throughout the neck, shoulders, and back, as these areas are commonly affected by stress.

- Fatigue after an event within our relationship can indicate a period of anxiety or being triggered before.

- Difficulty sleeping or experiencing sleep disturbances like nightmares, frequently waking up in the night, or restless sleep.

- Loss of appetite or relying on food as a source of comfort.

When was the last time you felt triggered and experienced some of these symptoms? Think about what came next and how your relationship was affected. The technique I'm about to share will help outcomes like that become a problem of the past. But first, let's talk about some triggers that are common in anxious attachment.

Common Triggers For Individuals With Anxious Attachment

It's helpful to pay attention to what happens within our relationships as we begin experiencing the triggered physiological or psychological responses. This can help us identify what our triggers are. Consider which triggers from this list sound and feel familiar:

- Conflict within a relationship, particularly arguments that go unresolved.
- Feeling or perceiving our partners pulling away emotionally.
- Physical distance between us and our partners.
- Having a partner leave for a business trip or vacation with others.
- Receiving negative feedback or criticism within the relationship.
- Unpredictable or inconsistent communication from our partners.

- Seeing our partners interact lovingly with others, even in appropriate settings.

- Any indication that our partners might want to leave us or are unsatisfied with the relationship.

- Moments where our partners forget or neglect to offer enough verbal or physical affection towards us, perhaps forgetting to kiss us goodbye, or hold a hug for as long as we'd like.

- When an expectation or need within the relationship goes unmet. For example, expecting our partners to text us 'good morning' and the corresponding trigger if they don't.

- Having family members come to stay in a shared home with our partners, where our quality time may be impeded.

- Things unrelated to the relationship that worsen anxiety levels, such as poor health or a change in circumstances.

Whether you experience any of these triggers or have identified some of your own triggers throughout this chapter, take a moment to visit your Workbook now and complete the exercise there. It will help you prepare for your next trigger moment.

I'd like you to know that you don't have to be absolutely clear on what your triggers are in order to heal. Many of us may have such a varied repertoire of triggers that it can be hard to keep track. What matters most is getting better at recognizing when we're triggered and managing how we respond.

YOUR TRIGGER RESPONSE PLAN

Being triggered puts our nervous system in a state of fight-or-flight, where we may not feel able to think logically or act from a grounded perspective.[51] This means that we are unable to self-regulate. Both our emotions and our behavior. So, we need a circuit breaker. A process to stop us from continuing The Self-Sabotage Cycle.

The EGO Response Technique

This technique is intended for the moment you realize you've experienced a trigger and are under the spell of the symptoms we've explored above. There are 3 simple steps to follow:

E - Encounter Your Triggers.

G - Ground Yourself

O - Own Your True Needs.

E - *Encounter Your Triggers*

Just acknowledging that you are encountering a trigger is a powerful interruption to the experience. This is where you begin to regain control.

G - *Ground Yourself*

Then, no matter what you're thinking, feeling, or about to say or do, stop. Pause for a moment to ground yourself. The easiest and most effective way is to simply take a long, deep breath.

E - Encounter Your Triggers.

G - Ground Yourself.

O - Own Your True Needs.

Alternatively, take a moment, leave the room, shake out your arms, get your bare feet on some grass, close your eyes, and imagine yourself swimming in the warm ocean.

These practices are simple and transformative. It is you in an act of self-soothing. It's you managing your nervous system in an effective, responsible way. It's you taking back control of your mind and body. It needs to be your first response the moment you identify the symptoms we've called out earlier.

O - *Own Your True Needs.*

Anxious attachment can overshadow our needs and cause us to try to fulfill them in unconventional or even manipulative ways. For example, we might tell our partner to leave us alone when our need is for connection.

Owning your needs will help you realign your thoughts, emotions, and behaviors with them. To do this, ask yourself: What am I needing right now?

Your answer may include one or more of the following:

- Closeness
- Emotional connection
- Feeling understood or heard
- Physical or emotional safety
- Validation
- Affection
- Reassurance
- Respect
- Intimacy
- Comfort

The EGO Response Technique is a quick way to acknowledge every aspect of the experience and bring the intensity down. In the Workbook, there is an exercise you can use to personalize the **EGO Response Technique** to ensure it works for you every time. We will each have a unique response to stress, which is why it's important to personalize this plan. Use the structure and see the suggested changes in the Workbook that you might prefer.

YOUR FIRST STEP TOWARD SECURITY IN RELATIONSHIPS

The first time I noticed my anxiety dissolving was during a terrible argument with my partner. Conflict was one of my biggest triggers, where I would become overwhelmed quickly and lose control. My heart was already pounding and there was a buzzing in my feet. I was already triggered but hadn't realized it yet. Then, within minutes, I noticed my partner's words start to blur into noise as my body surged with a violent energy. I was about to explode.

Just before I started shouting, all the hard work I'd put into understanding my behavior up until this point paid off. Like a distant thought, I remembered to breathe. Instead of letting my rage get the better of me, I stopped. I paused, blocking everything out for a moment, and took a deep breath. As I emptied my lungs, slowly blowing the air out through pursed lips, I realized that I was intensely triggered. I continued to breathe as I acknowledged my experience, feeling validated that everything was okay. I was triggered, and it made sense.

I asked myself why I felt triggered and what I needed in that moment – an emotional regulation tactic that I had learned in therapy and applied in other, less intense situations. I recognized that my urge to explode and shout came from feeling unheard and misunderstood. I wanted to shout with the intention of getting my partner to listen to me. But, instead of shouting, I had gained enough control to do things differently.

I'll never forget that argument because of the hard pill I had to swallow. After calming myself enough to prevent an explosion, the argument quickly blew over. It wasn't my partner who turned arguments into painful shouting matches. It was me. It was difficult to take responsibility for my actions. It was easier to just follow my instincts when I became triggered. However, addressing my triggers and learning to self-soothe in those heated moments empowered me to continue growing and healing, and my relationship benefitted immeasurably.

Now that you have a simple, effective plan for coping when triggered, use it to help you regain control before you think, feel, and do things that may damage your relationships.

In the next chapter, we will address the next stage in The Self-Sabotage Cycle: The harmful thinking patterns that amplify our pain and feed into our wounds.

Next, I'll get you prepared to face the thoughts keeping you trapped. They're not your fault, they're simply cognitive symptoms of anxious attachment that need to be addressed and can be reframed with one simple technique.

4

HOW TO REMOVE NEGATIVE THOUGHTS

Making Way For Kindness And Self-Compassion

"How people treat you is their karma; how you react is yours"

– Wayne Dyer

THE POWER OF YOUR THOUGHTS AND SELF-TALK

Thoughts can carry such weight. Enough weight to bring us to our knees. Without taking the proper care to manage and question our thoughts, we give them the power to rule our lives. But not all thoughts are equal. Some thoughts are grounded in truth, and some in fear or false beliefs. Learning to tell the difference can be difficult yet very powerful.

Many of the problems we face with anxious attachment are created by our thought patterns. Negative thought patterns, also known as cognitive distortions, can cause us to perceive problems that don't exist – thoughts that are not grounded in truth.[52] We can experience inner turmoil within our relationships, much of which our partners have little or nothing to do with. But thankfully, the cognitive (mind-based) symptoms of anxious attachment are where we have the most control.

We can develop a skill called cognitive reframing. A skill that allows us to take control of our thoughts so that they don't spoil our reality. It allows us to restructure, replace, or release thoughts that are only leading to unhelpful emotional experiences. Cognitive reframing is not about resisting negative thoughts or invalidating thoughts that reflect our true experiences.[53] It's about learning to view our thoughts from a more objective perspective so we can gain the freedom to either:

- choose them; or
- change them.

Our minds are like computers running a program of all the information we've been fed our entire lives. Change happens when we feed our minds new data by reframing the thoughts we don't want so that they slowly have less control and eventually disappear.

In this chapter, I'll demystify the most common negative thought patterns that are part of anxious attachment. These patterns come from unhealthy places within us and need to be managed for our own well-being. To do so, I'll share a simple technique that will empower you to take control of your thoughts for healthier outcomes in your relationships.

IDENTIFYING NEGATIVE THOUGHT PATTERNS

Cognitive distortions are the negative thought patterns that amplify negative emotions.[54] In anxious attachment, such thoughts can make us feel perpetually unhappy in our relationships and within ourselves. They can include:

- **Personalization:** Taking responsibility for events outside of your control like attributing negative outcomes to your actions. "My ex verbally abused me because I instigated arguments."

- **Overgeneralization:** Viewing a single negative event as a defeating cycle that never ends, ie., "I always screw up my relationships no matter what."

- **Black-and-white thinking:** Thinking in absolutes with no middle ground. "If my partner doesn't respond right away, they obviously don't care about me."

- **Fortune-telling:** Predicting negative outcomes without any real evidence. "My partner is going to leave me eventually, I just know it."

- **Catastrophizing:** Imagining the worst case scenario of a situation and feeling anxious that it will play out. "She's already 15 minutes late, what if she was in an accident."

- **Labeling:** Assigning a negative label to yourself or others based on specific observations or events without any real considerations, knowledge, or long-term evidence. "Because my partner doesn't give me enough affection, I must be unlovable."

- **Comparison:** Measuring the health and success of our relationships against others. "Mary got engaged after 2 years with her boyfriend, why hasn't Jack proposed yet if we've been together for longer?"

- **Magnification or minimization:** Blowing situations out of proportion or minimizing their importance. "My partner not texting me back is unforgivable." or "I really need more affection, but what does it matter anyway."

- **Disqualifying positives:** Failing to acknowledge or accept positive experiences. "That was the best date I've ever had, but it still doesn't mean they like me."

- **Jumping to conclusions:** Making quick negative assumptions about a situation without evidence to support them. "He's working late again, of course he's found someone else."

- **Should-ing and must-ing:** Placing ourselves or our relationships under unfair or unnecessary pressure by creating rigid rules or standards about how we or they should function. "I should never have put my heart on the line." or "We must not fight anymore."[55]

Can you relate to any of these? I know too well how most of these feel. I've seen their destructive impact on my relationships and on myself. So, let me show you the tools required for reframing such negative thoughts to make sure you and your relationships don't suffer as I have. We'll start with the simple habit of kindness.

KINDNESS: A KEY PART OF YOUR HEALING

I've been a people-pleaser for most of my life, willingly self-sacrificing to win the approval of others. In relationships, I was always someone others could rely on to say yes, help out, do my part, and then some. I was running on empty, filling cups with whatever energy I could muster. This might seem noble, but beneath the surface, there was something more sinister: fear. Deep down, I tried my best not to take up space or be a burden on anyone out of a fear of losing them – a fear that fueled my anxious attachment.

As I began healing, I started asking more questions about my behavior and noticed more patterns, both in and out of relationships. I started observing my thoughts and quickly learned why I self-sacrificed and self-sabotaged so much.

My thoughts were critical, harsh, and unforgiving. I'd catch myself thinking things like, "Gosh, I'm such an idiot!", "If only I could do something right for once." and "Maybe if I could be fitter/dress better/act differently, then I'd be worth the effort." The way I was treating myself was borderline abusive. If a partner were to speak to me the way I spoke to myself, I would never believe that they loved me. And that was where the penny dropped.

I didn't love myself.

When we don't love ourselves, we feel impatient, angry, or apathetic towards ourselves, leading to a host of unhelpful or even hurtful thoughts. We may hold ourselves to unrealistic standards and feel frustrated at ourselves when we don't live up to them. Our level of self-love correlates to our self-worth. Because anxious attachment can come from a place of low self-worth, "Do I love myself?" is a great question for us to ask.

When we are anxiously attached, it might feel counterintuitive to stop seeking love and validation externally and offering it to ourselves instead. But showing ourselves compassion and building a sense of self-love is an essential part of our healing journey. It reaches through the noise of anxious attachment and begins to heal us at the core. It helps us become self-fulfilled.

We set the standard for how we deserve to be loved. Although it might feel strange at first or even completely foreign, practicing self-compassion can improve our lives and relationships enormously.[56] There are 3 components to self-compassion that can quickly shift your perspective about yourself. Let's explore them.

The 3 Components Of Self-Compassion

Self-compassion is when we extend kindness, understanding, and support to ourselves, especially when we feel bad, fail at something, or self-sabotage. Pioneered by research psychologist Dr. Kristin Neff, the 3 components of self-compassion include:[57]

Self-Kindness

This is when we choose to treat ourselves with warmth and gentleness rather than harsh criticism and judgment. In anxious attachment, we might choose to self-soothe rather than beat ourselves up for getting triggered in relationships. We might talk to ourselves in a kind and soothing tone, using our words and thoughts to help us work through hard times. We might decide to honor our needs instead of people-pleasing or self-sacrificing.

Common Humanity

When we're in the midst of a challenging circumstance, it can be easy to forget that struggles are a normal part of life. Common humanity is the realization that we aren't alone in our suffering, mistakes, or imperfections. It's breaking away from feelings of isolation and connecting to the collective human experience instead.

In anxious attachment, understanding common humanity can help us let go of the belief that we are flawed or deserving of our struggles. It may help us to gain a more realistic perspective of things, helping to heal cognitive distortions like minimization and magnification, personalization, comparison, and many others. We can recognize that our difficulties are understandable and normal. Having an anxious attachment style doesn't make us broken or wrong, it is a part of our life's journey. Working to heal insecure attachment is about learning to love ourselves because we deserve to feel good, not because we are flawed.

Mindfulness

Mindfulness is the component that makes the first two possible. It gives us the ability to approach our healing mindfully. Without it, we might struggle to see the point of self-compassion and stay stuck in negative thinking patterns that block us from achieving self-love.

As we heal, mindfulness can help us be present in our relationships, more realistic about our expectations, and ultimately more regulated and secure in our thoughts and emotions. It can bring us to a more stable mental space where we feel capable of cognitive reframing.

Self-compassion can help us build a strong sense of self-love, recognize our worth, and face cognitive distortions in a gentle and effective way. The technique we will explore next requires a willingness to break old patterns and do what's best for ourselves in the toughest times. It's known as the ERS Technique, and I still use it regularly to keep my thoughts in check.

NEW, BETTER THOUGHTS

Thoughts, emotions, and behaviors often happen simultaneously, which can make cognitive reframing difficult. Anxiety, rage, and other painful emotions can keep us in a continuous loop of negative thinking, as they may override our systems and make thinking clearly or rationally feel impossible.

Mindfulness can help us ground and stay present for long enough to see our thoughts more objectively. It helps us be our own heroes, saving ourselves from intense negative experiences. Instead of allowing anxiety to make us worry about the future or fixate on the past, mindfulness allows us to focus on what's happening right in front of us.

Once we've experienced a trigger that may have already created negative thinking and painful emotions, we need to find powerful and effective ways to ground ourselves quickly before they lead to protest behaviors. Your immediate approach is the EGO Response Technique from Chapter 3.

The EGO Technique is the 'first responder' on the scene of a trigger. It's your go-to approach. It's the equivalent of an ambulance arriving, without which there could be a fatality!

However, my next technique is part of your ongoing health plan so you require the services of the relationship paramedics less and less.

We don't want to just be adept at navigating our triggers. Instead, we want to encounter them less frequently. So, here is another simple technique that will cause a profound shift in the way your thoughts govern the health of your relationships: the **ERS Technique**.

E: Examine your Thoughts

R: Replace Your Thoughts

S: Self-Compassion Through Mindfulness.

E - Examine your Thoughts.

R - Replace Your Thoughts.

S - Self-Compassion Through Mindfulness.

ERS can help you dissolve persistent negative thought patterns and reframe your thoughts using mindfulness tools.

Plus, because we're reframing our thoughts from a place of self-compassion, we will not only feel better immediately but we'll also cultivate a healthier long-term relationship with our thoughts.[58]

E - Examine your Thoughts

Making time to investigate our thoughts can help us process them, recognize any cognitive distortions, and let them go.

As an example, anxious attachment can cause us to enact self-sabotage behaviors. To interrupt this pattern, we can examine our thoughts with the following questions:

- Are my thoughts accurate? Are they helpful?
- How are they making me feel?
- If I had to share these thoughts with someone I trust, what might they say?
- What advice would I give a close friend having the same thoughts?
- What can I learn from these thoughts?
- Is there a need hiding behind these thoughts?

In your Workbook, there is space for you to answer these questions the next time you feel stuck in a negative thinking pattern. You can also complete this exercise using a past experience. This will help you understand what went wrong and how you can make the next experience better for you and your partner. Turn to your Workbook and complete this now.

R - Reframe Your Thoughts

Once we have a clear idea of the negative thought patterns we find ourselves in, we can begin to reframe our thoughts. This is not just about being positive, it's about helping our thoughts reflect truth. For example, neutralizing a negative thought can look like:

- "I'm such an idiot!" to "I feel like an idiot for behaving that way, but I didn't know better. Next time, I'll do things differently." This went from **labeling** to understanding and forgiving.

- "My relationships keep failing, I'm going to be single and alone forever." Instead: "My relationships keep failing, perhaps I'm not choosing the right partners." or "My relationships keep failing, perhaps I need to focus on myself for a while to understand my behavior." This went from **catastrophizing** to more realistic, solution-orientated thinking.

- "They never buy me gifts, it's obvious they don't care about me." to "They did take me out for a nice dinner last week, I think I'm just feeling underappreciated this week because they've been very busy at work. Maybe I'll plan something nice for us to do together." This went from **overgeneralization** and **jumping to conclusions** to investigating the evidence, finding a need, and offering a solution.

Your Workbook will guide you through a personalized approach to this using your own thoughts.

S - Self-Compassion Through Mindfulness

Finally, take time to develop self-compassion through mindfulness activities. These quick mindfulness activities are a great way to soothe ourselves after working through negative thoughts, pick one each time you run this ERS Technique:

- **Practice gratitude:** Think of one good thing that happened in your relationship recently and smile as you allow gratitude to lift your mood. Use this activity for the times when you may feel negative about your partner or the relationship.

- **Reflect on your strengths:** Name one good thing about yourself as a partner or friend. Perhaps you're very loving, give the best gifts, or maybe you always show up on time for important dates and events. Use this activity when your cognitive distortions are breaking down your self-worth or self-image.

- **Visualize a positive outcome:** Take a moment to visualize how a previous situation could have gone with your new thoughts in place. Become comfortable with images of successful interactions, resolved arguments, and warmth in your relationship. Use this activity if your cognitive distortions create a lot of anxiety about the future, or if they fixate on hurtful past events.

With the ERS Technique, you have a simple yet powerful tool to begin creating thoughts that help instead of harm. It's a technique you can use daily, weekly, or any time you feel like you need to give yourself a cognitive boost.

Practice it now. Go to your Workbook, and I'll walk you through a quick session. It's easy, and once you're done, you'll feel your personal energy humming at a higher tone.

Did you do that? I hope so. It's incredibly valuable.

If so, how do you feel? Do you see yourself in the near future, feeling at peace and far more secure in your relationships? That's where I want you to find yourself. Please know that it is possible. I and hundreds of others who have read these pages know that it is.

One more point about thoughts – the thoughts we have regularly can create a harmful internal narrative. I'll show you how to shift that into an inner voice that is kind, supportive, and uplifting.

REWRITING YOUR INNER NARRATIVE

Many of the negative thoughts that accompany an anxious attachment come from false beliefs. Such beliefs are often generated by our attachment wounds.

The negative thoughts stemming from a false belief can provoke a critical, self-deprecating, or anxious inner voice. Some false beliefs at the root of that destructive little voice may include:

- I'm not good enough.
- I'm unlovable.
- People will leave me.

- I need others to feel complete.
- I can't trust others.
- I'm always going to feel abandoned.
- My needs aren't important.
- I have to earn love and approval.
- I can't handle being alone.
- I'm too needy.
- I will be rejected if I show my true self.
- I am a burden to others.
- I must always be available to others.
- Conflict means they don't love me.
- I can't rely on anyone.
- Relationships clearly aren't for me.

Limiting beliefs like these can have grave consequences because, like a filter, they may alter our perception of life. Our beliefs can determine how happy we perceive ourselves to be in relationships regardless of circumstances.[59]

They may also lead to experiences that continue to reinforce them. For example, when we believe "I'm too needy," we may begin a push-pull dynamic that causes more anxiety, creating more feelings of desperation and neediness.

As we cultivate self-compassion and begin understanding our anxious attachment, we may begin to uncover these beliefs and gain the awareness to change them. Once we've identified a false belief, we can choose a new, more helpful belief and use our thoughts to reinforce it.

Positive affirmations are another powerful cognitive reframing tool useful for shifting false beliefs.[60] For example, to improve our anxious attachment, we might use the affirmation "I can support myself" to shift the belief "I need others to feel complete." In the Workbook, there is an exercise to help you identify the false beliefs behind your inner voice and a list of helpful affirmations to try. Take a moment to work through the activity before we move on.

CONCLUSION

Cognitive distortions are a very real and heavy aspect of anxious attachment that can lead to painful emotions and damaging behaviors. Self-compassion is a key tool we can use to accept these thinking patterns and begin transforming them with the reframing tools we've learned.

As we effectively manage our thoughts, our emotions and behaviors will improve. However, we can take our healing much further. Painful emotions are a force to contend with. When you're ready, join me in Chapter 5, where we will discuss the next component of the Self-Sabotage Cycle and learn to become our own heroes in emotionally intense times.

5

STRONG MIND, STRONG RELATIONSHIPS

Building Emotional Resilience
And Intelligence

"Each relationship nurtures a strength or weakness within you."

– Mike Murdock

THOUGHTS, BEHAVIOR, EMOTIONAL STRENGTH

There was a feeling of hopelessness that would linger for hours and occasionally days after an argument. My thoughts would fixate on the worst-case outcome, and I'd lie on the couch watching TV for hours every night to escape my anxiety. Sometimes, I'd fall asleep in the living room to avoid a sleepless night alone in bed. Until I could reconnect with my partner and resolve things between us, it felt difficult for me to find a sense of peace or stability on my own. Even though I had become able to *tolerate* intense negative emotions, I hadn't built the skills required to *cope* with them. I always relied on my partner to rescue me from despair after an argument.

I'm naturally an empathetic person, but once triggered, my negative thinking patterns and intense emotions would trap me in The Self-Sabotage Cycle, where I would lose a sense of reality about my relationship. My insecurities would take precedence, and I'd become a victim. I'd struggle to empathize with my partner appropriately, either blaming him for my pain or taking responsibility for his.

Even though I was a loving person in relationships, I had a lot to learn about emotional intelligence. The empathy and care I showed to others when they were having a tough time seemed to fall aside when I felt dysregulated. I'd become needy and accusatory yet difficult to console. There was no room for resolution when I was in this state, even though I expected others to console me.

As I pursued learning and growth, determined not to ruin the good relationship I was in, I was encouraged by early signs of real progress. I started acknowledging my behavior and managing that more effectively through the EGO Technique. I enjoyed watching the positive impact on my relationship.

I took the steps to reframe my negative thoughts as I regularly ran through the ERS Technique. I not only started feeling hopeful about the future of my relationship, but I also felt a strength growing in my sense of self.

However, there was another personal domain I had yet to conquer.

I had the tools to manage my behavior and my thoughts, but I knew it was equally important to address my emotions.[61]

For those with anxious attachment, emotions can be particularly overwhelming, often leading to regrettable actions or a desperate need for support. This chapter introduces a technique to help you:

- Process emotions effectively
- Develop new, healthier coping mechanisms
- Build emotional intelligence for better relationships

It's called the **Calm Coping Technique**.

This tool will help you replace old emotional patterns with more effective ones, regardless of past experiences. It has been instrumental in my own journey, and I know it can support you on yours.

UNDERSTANDING AND MANAGING OUR EMOTIONS

Emotional intelligence is about understanding and managing our emotions.[62] Healing anxious attachment requires a level of emotional intelligence that allows us to face conflict with more emotional security.

Rather than fixating on our internal experience, we can become more objective. We can soothe our own emotions and better empathize with others. For instance, you might spiral into anxiety when your partner doesn't respond to your text within an hour, imagining scenarios where they're ignoring you or have lost interest. Or you might feel overwhelmed with jealousy when you see your partner laughing with a coworker at a company event, even though, logically, you know it's an innocent interaction. This is completely understandable when you're anxiously attached.

So, here is the **Calm Coping Technique**. An easy and effective way to lower the intensity of any emotion and build the emotional resilience needed to cope. It has 3 simple steps:

Step 1: Recognize And Label The Emotions

If we don't stop and ask ourselves which emotions we're experiencing, managing them is impossible. We need to be able to recognize what we're feeling and acknowledge these emotions. There is a lot of power in stating "I feel angry" when we're angry.

When you notice **symptoms** of an emotion, such as a tight chest, warmth in the body, or negative thoughts, take a moment to identify the emotion as best as possible. You can compare the feeling to past experiences, notice what urges come with it, and then choose a label that best suits it.

To accurately label our emotions, start with the 7 primary emotions: happiness, sadness, 'bad' emotions, fear, surprise, disgust, and anger. These emotions can extend into more nuanced emotional experiences, as you'll see from the chart below.

Before you move on to the next section, take a moment with the exercise in your Workbook for a visualization exercise that will help you practice identifying emotions when they happen.

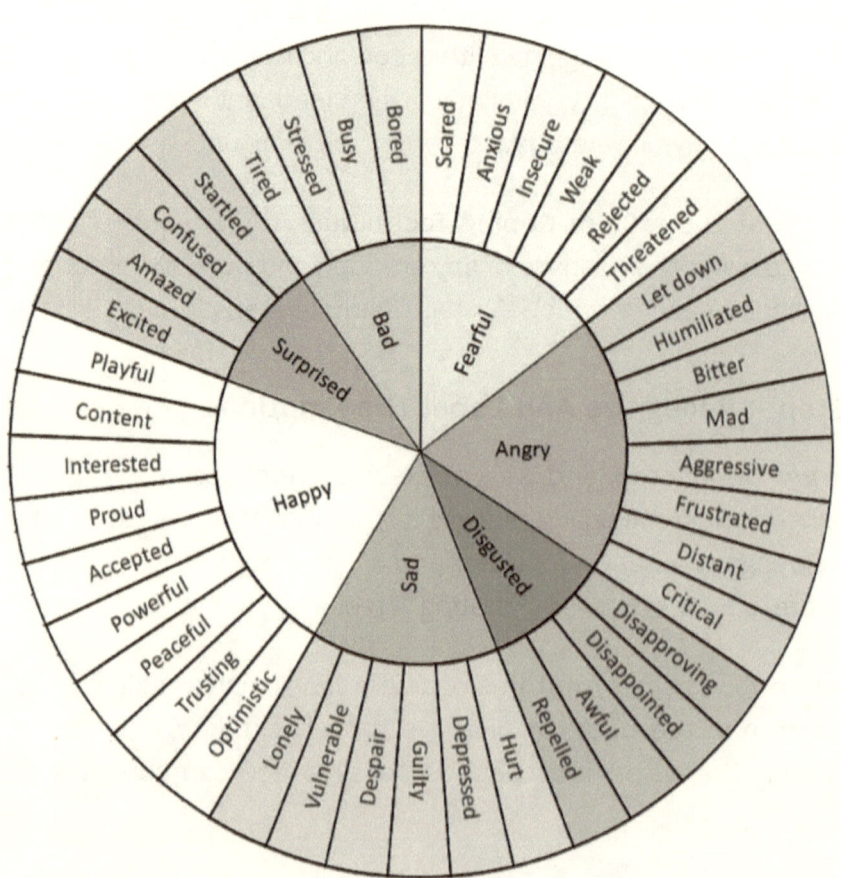

Step 2: Apply A Coping Skill To Regulate

If the emotion is particularly intense, we should hopefully have applied the EGO Technique to regain control of our behavior. Now, we can take that a step further and use a coping technique to fully regulate the emotion. Regulating an emotion means returning to a more balanced and calm state.[63]

Depending on the emotion we're experiencing, we can choose an activity that will be effective for the state we're in. For example, if we're angry, we may choose a more physical activity, and if we're sad, we might allow ourselves to indulge in a healthy comfort. Some coping skills proven to regulate intense emotions and build a stronger foundation of calm include:

Getting Active In A Fun And Uplifting Way

Exercise is one of the most effective tools for lifting our moods.[64] Why not use it to help relieve the emotional intensity associated with anxious attachment? We can take a walk through the park, put some music on and dance, or head to the gym. We can even invite our partners along for quicker, more effective conflict resolution.[65]

Taking Some Alone Time To Express The Emotion

We don't have to keep our emotions to ourselves to stay regulated. Expressing them in a way that fully satisfies the emotion can often be more effective.[66] What's important is that our expression is constructive and not harmful to ourselves or others. Some useful regulation strategies that allow for full expression include:

- **Pillow slams:** A therapeutic technique effective at releasing anger or frustration. In this technique, we throw a pillow down onto the floor with some force.

- **Expressive journaling:** A powerful journal exercise in which we write down how we feel and what's on our minds without any filter. This exercise is in your Workbook. Give it a try!

- **Crying:** Crying is our body's natural regulating response. It has been proven to help us soothe emotional distress, feel less pain, and more.[67]

Distract Yourself With A Healthy Activity

Distraction isn't always an unhealthy coping strategy. In the face of intense, painful emotions, we may need to engage in an activity that takes our minds off our stress. What matters is that the activity is enjoyable and productive rather than something destructive like a night out drinking or watching excessive TV.

This technique is particularly helpful when we're stuck in a negative thinking pattern that is creating a host of negative feelings. For example, if your anxiety is ramped up while your partner is on a business trip, it may be more helpful to sign up for a craft class or go see a friend instead of reaching out to your partner for comfort.

Do Something Relaxing

Relaxation techniques can be very effective in the face of intense emotions. Giving ourselves the time and space to calmly overcome the emotion can be incredibly powerful. We can simply surrender to the way we feel and wait for it to pass mindfully. You might consider trying:

- **Deep breathing:** Spend 5-10 minutes just focusing on taking long, slow, deep breaths.
- **Wall sits:** Lie on your back with your feet up against the wall, allowing your body to sink into the floor while your mind rests.
- **Basic self-care:** Take a bath with some essential oils, listen to gentle music, eat a nourishing meal, and watch an uplifting movie.

The effectiveness of **The Calm Coping Technique** lies in choosing the exercises that work best for you. If relaxation techniques help you most, do those! If your anger gets the better of you, get active! However, you don't have to have it all figured out right now. What matters is that you try things that will help you regulate in a healthier way and figure out what brings you back to calm the quickest.

It's important to manage our emotions before we engage with others. We don't need to be fully calm to manage this well, but we need to feel balanced enough to show empathy, which is an essential part of emotional intelligence.

THE TOOLKIT

With consistent effort, we can move away from destructive emotional patterns and improve our emotional balance for healthier relationships. We now have 3 easy and effective techniques for breaking free from The Self-Sabotage Cycle:

- **The EGO Technique:** A first response to triggers and the best way to manage our **behavior** in the heat of the moment.

- **The ERS Technique:** Secondary support for addressing and shifting negative **thinking** patterns and beliefs.

- **The Calm Coping Technique:** A long-term approach to developing coping skills in the face of painful **emotions**.

With these techniques in our toolkit, we can take meaningful, practical steps to building healthier, more secure relationships.

When you're ready, meet me in Part 3, Chapter 6, where we will explore the foundation of the securely attached person – a strong sense of self. This will allow us to show up stronger in relationships.

PART 3

IMPROVING YOUR RELATIONSHIPS

6

HOW TO BE STRONG

4 Methods To Restore Your Strength In Relationships

"We are afraid to care too much, for fear that the other person does not care at all."

–Eleanor Roosevelt

CREATING A STRONG SENSE OF SELF

As people with anxious attachment, we may feel perplexed by the rejection, criticism, and relationship failures we face. And although we tend to blame ourselves, we may not realize why we're at fault. The fault is not in our worth or ability to love, it's in our lack of authenticity. When we don't live our lives loving who we are and expressing our true nature, it becomes impossible for others to recognize our value. After all, how can they recognize something they rarely get to see?

Just think about what anxious attachment does to you. Can you agree that it's very much rooted in fears and wounds? Operating from a place of fear in our lives causes us to show up as a shadow of who we truly are. We're not generating fulfilling, loving experiences, we're just trying to survive.

When we have low self-worth and a lack of self-love, we may struggle to realize how great we are. We may fixate on our weaknesses, overlooking or underplaying our strengths in relationships. We may not see the value in our own ideas and understanding, so we rely on others for validation. However, when we're not being authentic, the validation we might get can feel hollow.

If we were to identify our true values and beliefs and commit to being an authentic expression of these, no matter the impact on our relationships, we would be living true to ourselves and attracting partners who truly appreciate us for who we are, fostering deeper, more meaningful connections and ultimately leading to greater fulfillment and happiness in our relationships and in life.

In this chapter, we will get **very** clear about our core values and beliefs and learn how to display them in relationships with confidence. We will also learn how to take our confidence inward so we can accept ourselves and realize how great we are. If we want others to love and appreciate our value, we have to get clear on who we are and make sure we express that honestly.

I want you to feel so strong in yourself that everything you say and do becomes an authentic expression. That way, your authentic behavior will no longer align with the flow of the Self-Sabotage Cycle.

GALVANIZE YOUR CORE VALUES AND BELIEFS

Getting clear on our values and beliefs and then allowing ourselves to stand by them can completely transform the way we show up in the world and in relationships. To get clear on our authentic values and beliefs, we need to learn what makes us want to passionately stand up and say, "Yes!" or "No. That's Not OK!"

We may feel in our hearts what our values are but not have the right words to articulate them. Reflect on each of these values and consider which ones are most important to you:

- **Trust:** Believing in the reliability, truth, and capability of our partners.

- **Respect:** Valuing others' beliefs, boundaries, and individuality.

- **Empathy:** Understanding and showing care toward others' emotions.

- **Honesty:** Being truthful and transparent in our interactions with others

- **Loyalty:** Being faithful and supportive through the highs and lows.

- **Patience:** Staying calm and understanding in the face of challenges and differences.

- **Open Communication:** The open and honest exchange of thoughts, feelings, and information.

- **Commitment:** Showing dedication to a relationship and having a willingness to work through conflict.

There is an extension of this list with a few key exercises in your Workbook to help you get clear on your core values and beliefs. When we choose and stay in relationships that match our values, we can significantly reduce the chances of having our boundaries crossed and furthering our anxiety in relationships. We can honor who we are and attract the right people into our lives.

I know this is easier said than done. There are more steps needed to actively stand by our core values and beliefs and build a secure sense of self. This is where I'd like to guide you through some simple steps to becoming confident in who you are and asserting that.

SELF-CONFIDENT AND ASSERTIVE

I can recall a time when my sense of self was so diminished by an unhealthy relationship that I didn't even recognize myself. I didn't feel strong enough to stand up for myself when he insulted me or remove myself from situations where I felt unsafe. My self-esteem was at rock-bottom, so I stayed in this situation for years. Even though my mental health was deteriorating, I was so scared of being alone and fully believed no one else would love me. I believed this was what I deserved.

After getting the professional help I needed to rebuild my self-esteem and escape this relationship, I'm happy to say that I was completely wrong. I found love again, and it was nothing like what I had experienced before. It was whole, expansive, and beautiful. But I hadn't healed enough to fully accept it as something I deserved. My anxious behavior continued to cause conflict and push the relationship away until I changed. I did the things I'm going to suggest to you and it completely transformed my presence in relationships.

The things I'm going to suggest will help you become unapologetically comfortable with who you are so you can find the self-confidence to assert your needs in a healthy way. They're going to help you recognize your value and teach you how to convey that value to others so that you attract the relationships you truly deserve.

We owe it to ourselves to stop feeling miserable in our relationships. We don't have to let anxious attachment rule our lives or define who we are. But anxious attachment can have a grip that is difficult to escape without guts.

Secure people manage to stay out of the lows we may face in relationships because they don't waste time trying to be someone they're not. They wake up with a strong sense of who they are, and they bring it. No matter what. They don't wonder whether they're good enough, they know they are. Secure people are confident in themselves, independent of their personality type or the opinions of others.[68]

Self-confidence is not about being extroverted or charismatic. It's the ability to own our true nature and allow ourselves to be seen.[69] When we can wake up ready to live our truths without worrying about what others may think or trying to be someone we're not, self-confidence is a natural consequence of authenticity.

Strategies For Boosting Self-Confidence

Our anxious attachment style means we may put on a mask that matches who we think others want us to be to avoid rejection or criticism. But doing this can eliminate our authenticity and lead to a decline in our self-esteem – the opposite of self-confidence.

To boost our self-confidence, we need to become more secure in who we are and be ready to let our authenticity breathe. To do this, we can:

Own Our Quirks

Each one of us is beautifully unique. To boost our self-confidence, it's important that we are willing to accept our wonderful quirks and recognize that it's okay to be superbly different. As people who grew up experiencing anxious attachment, we may be more sensitive, highly empathetic, and more willing to work on ourselves. We may have quirks that we later discover to be strengths.[70]

Speak Our Truth

The things we say can form part of the anxious masks we wear to fit in and be liked. We may alter our opinions and reduce our thoughts to match what we think others want to hear. But this can be detrimental to our sense of identity as it may lead us to disregard our values and beliefs for the sake of others.

To feel good about who we are and practice self-confidence, we need to speak our truth, even if it may lead to conflict at times. If how we feel is the honest truth, then others can either accept it or move on. Remember what I said about this taking guts? This is when you need to prioritize your truth over others' comfort. Can you do that?

Spend Time Building Ourselves Up

We may have spent years focusing on being the perfect partner without considering what we actually like. We may have started listening to certain music, dressing a certain way, or taking up hobbies that align with someone else's ideal partner. Where does your authentic self fit into this picture?

Self-confidence is a natural consequence of doing things that make us feel good about ourselves. If we love who we are and feel proud of the things we do, it's easier to feel comfortable in our characters. This may require that we take up new hobbies or acquire new skills that we are genuinely interested in. If who we are right now doesn't inspire self-confidence, it's okay to spend time figuring out what we like and reestablishing ourselves up with hobbies or skills we are passionate about.

Become More Assertive

As our self-confidence builds, we may find ourselves becoming more assertive naturally. But assertiveness can feel aggressive when we aren't used to standing up for who we are and what we believe. Don't let that stop you. To support our growth and become more assertive, we can:

- Assert our boundaries and beliefs when appropriate.
- Manage our emotions to stay calm and composed.
- Practice clear and concise communication.
- Use strong posture and good eye contact.
- Be direct and honest when sharing opinions.
- Get comfortable saying "No."

It's incredibly powerful to feel so secure in ourselves that the desire to fit in and be liked just doesn't matter anymore. This is when we know we love ourselves fully. There isn't anything anyone can say to break our self-confidence because we have already owned and embraced our identity, flaws, warts, and all.

From this inner sense of security, we can continue developing our strength and stave off unhealthy relationships like the one I used to be in. We can also use it to establish healthy relationship dynamics with good, loving partners. Keep reading, and I'll show you how.

STRENGTH THROUGH INDEPENDENCE

Finding strength within ourselves to grow out of old patterns and thrive in life can feel intimidating to do on our own. The wounds of anxious attachment may instigate beliefs that we can't rely on ourselves and that we need others in more ways than we truly do.

These wounds can keep us dependent on others in unhealthy ways. Much like I felt dependent on my unhealthy relationship to avoid being alone. We may become stuck in co-dependent relationships more easily, where we play into unhealthy relationship dynamics that keep us tied to people who may not be good for us.[71]

Relying on our relationships for support is normal and healthy. However, it can become a problem when relationships are our only source of support. We should always be our first line of support in life. We are the only person who is guaranteed to be there for us consistently, so it's important that we are strong and capable enough to support ourselves independently.

Co-dependence is a relationship dynamic that can be closely linked to anxious attachment.[72] It's a type of unhealthy relationship in which one person may self-sacrifice or give too much to a relationship out of a fear of losing it, while the other person becomes reliant on the extra support and care. This reliance enables the second person to continue bad behavior or stagnate in their personal growth.

In co-dependent relationships, we tend to give too much while our partners become reliant on our excessive support and clinginess. Then, as we grow and decide to heal, we may find our partners feeling confused or neglected as we take more time for ourselves.[73] Co-dependency is unsustainable and destructive for both parties as neither one is receiving a healthy amount of care and support to encourage growth.

To stave off co-dependence and reclaim a strong sense of identity, it's crucial that we prioritize autonomy in our relationships. Autonomy is the ability to be self-governed and independent, maintaining a sense of control over our own lives. Relationships should never dictate who we are and what we do with our lives. Of course, they can influence who we become and what we decide to do, but the influence should always be positive if the relationship is healthy. It should not be at the center of our lives, only complimentary to it.[74]

As anxiously attached people, we absolutely cannot continue to self-sacrifice if we want to have healthy relationships. Autonomy is a force that we can use to gain the strong sense of self we need. It will allow us to pursue our goals and personal interests without guilt or worry that the time spent focused on ourselves will interfere with our relationships.

Prioritizing Autonomy To Gain Independence

To develop a strong sense of self using the power of autonomy, there are two very important things we need to do:

- Pursue personal interests and goals, even if they take time away from our relationships.

- Embrace lifelong self-development, even if that means outgrowing relationships that hold us back.

Developing autonomy and building a strong sense of identity requires a level of commitment to growth that can feel selfish. Anxious attachment generally creates a self-sacrificing identity.[75] It ties our sense of well-being in with the satisfaction of others. That's why we need to let go of the fear of being selfish and commit ourselves to self-development. We need to learn to put ourselves first to balance the dynamics we normally create.

For example:

- If we cancel our plans with friends every time our partners ask us to do something else, we might practice saying no to our partners and make sure we maintain our friendships.

- If we neglect our own needs to jump on any opportunity we get to be with our partners, such as staying home with our partners instead of heading to the gym, we might choose to prioritize our needs above our partners desires and practice letting our partners down.

- If we abandon our hobbies whenever our partners want to spend time together, we might set aside specific times dedicated to our hobbies and ask our partners to respect that.

- If we compromise on our career aspirations to accommodate our partners schedules and desires, we might start prioritizing our professional development by being clear with our partners about when we need to focus on work.

- If we often neglect our self-care routines because we want to be available for our partners, we might practice discipline and stick to our self-care routine even if it inconveniences our partners sometimes.

To become secure with a strong sense of self, we need to be okay with taking up space. We need to accept that we will inconvenience others sometimes to stay on track with our health. We need to be able to say no to honor our needs and true desires. Loving ourselves must become our priority above all else.

You've made so much progress to get to this point, now it's time to embrace the journey toward becoming more secure and resilient. I need you to know that it's possible to erode anxious attachment and make room for more secure behaviors. Just keep going.

A SECURE AND RESILIENT SELF

As our behavior moves further from the flow of the Self-Sabotage Cycle and we begin building or reclaiming our sense of identity, we can show up in relationships as our authentic selves. Rather than self-effacing in relationships, we can begin to take up space in a way that helps us feel seen and heard. We can push through the discomfort of saying no, disappointing others, and the risk of losing people in order to honor our needs.

Becoming secure and resilient in our identity is a life-long journey that requires commitment and upkeep. We need to continue dedicating time to growth and autonomy. Anxious attachment is riddled with patterns that are easy to fall back into if we allow ourselves to.

Self-love and care must remain our top priorities if we are going to stay secure in ourselves and create sustainable relationships.

We must become our first line of reliable support before turning to others.

Being assertive and actively managing ourselves in relationships, no matter what others think, takes guts. However, the more you practice these behaviors, the more your comfort zone can expand to meet the parameters of secure attachment.

In the next chapter, we will continue to expand our comfort zones and learn the vital communication skills needed to set boundaries and sustain balanced connections. Meet me there. There are wonderful things to come!

7

POWERFUL COMMUNICATING AND CLEAR BOUNDARIES

How And Where To Draw The Line In Your Relationships

"No is a complete sentence."
– Annie Lamott

HEALTHY COMMUNICATION AND BOUNDARIES

In this chapter, I'll demonstrate how you can continue to adopt more secure behaviors by developing a secure communication style. I'll help you clarify your boundaries and encourage you to enforce them. Then, we will explore a powerful conflict resolution strategy.

You'll soon feel the comfort that comes from resolving an argument using secure communication. There'll be no need for tension, anxiety, or disconnection, and you won't feel the threat of your relationship dissolving. But first, we need to take a look at ineffective communication styles and the damage they can do.

Understanding Our Communication Style

One of the most painful stages of the Self-Sabotage Cycle is 'Damaged Relationships', which is almost invariably preceded by a round of awful communication.

People with anxious attachment often develop unhealthy communication habits. They may communicate indirectly, dismiss their partner's feelings, or express themselves excessively. This approach stems from a desire to get their needs met, but it often neglects the overall health of the relationship. As a result, these communication patterns can create significant tension between partners. When we fail to express ourselves clearly or maintain a positive connection, both individuals in the relationship may end up feeling unheard and unsatisfied.

We need to become aware of the way we use our words and body language to get our attachment needs met. With an anxious communication style, we are likely to:

- **Use passive-aggressive body language** to guilt trip, make an unhealthy bid for connection, or communicate dissatisfaction. For example, crossing our arms and sighing even though we've said nothing is wrong in an attempt to prompt further investigation.

- **Overapologize** even when we aren't responsible for a situation in an attempt to avoid conflict. For example, apologizing excessively after making a minor mistake that might upset our partners.

- **Ask excessive questions** to gain reassurance or validation. For example asking things like "Do you still love me? Are you sure?" on a regular basis.

- **Use indirect communication** to hint at our needs or feelings. For example, saying, "I guess we don't have to spend Saturday together if you're too busy." rather than "I'd love to spend Saturday together. Could you plan for some quality time?"

- **Use "always" and "never"** to over-exaggerate a problem. For example, saying, "You never buy me flowers." or "We always have to go places you suggest and we never go where I want to go." Most of the time, saying "always" or "never" is not realistic or fair.

- **Be dishonest about our feelings**, minimizing them to avoid causing our partners discomfort. For example, saying, "I'm fine" or saying that we feel the same way our partners do to avoid having to disagree with them.

Anxious communication can be dishonest and manipulative. We use our words and body language to stay small and safe in our relationships. However, rather than helping us feel more secure, it can further our relationship anxiety. It can cause significant damage to our relationships as we continue to be dishonest, self-sacrificing, and emotionally draining.

A secure communication style is an essential skill necessary for thriving relationships. It's clear, assertive, and empathetic. With an understanding of what secure communication looks like, we can unlearn our anxious communication style and replace it with communication that gets our needs met in a constructive way. There are 4 aspects of secure communication I'll share with you. They are what allowed me to stop hurting my relationships and experience the bliss of proper conflict resolution.

CREATING A SECURE COMMUNICATION STYLE

A secure communication style allows us to face conflict confidently, set boundaries, and feel satisfied in our relationships. It helps us communicate our needs and boundaries effectively, which is more likely to attract the results we want. It's also more likely to provide the security and understanding our partners need from us.

We can be honest without being hurtful, empathetic without self-sacrificing, and assertive without engaging in protest behaviors.

Secure communication doesn't require perfection. There have been plenty of times when I've slipped up and let my old communication patterns surface. What's important is that we understand how to regain connection and move forward.

Secure communication allows us to focus on:

- **Intentional statements and communication.** For example, secure people will reserve apologies for times when they are truly warranted, making them more impactful.

- **Direct communication of needs and emotions.** For example, rather than using body language to try and send a message, a secure person might say, "I feel hurt by what you said. Can we take a moment together and find a way to avoid this happening again?"

- **Clarity and understanding.** If a secure person doesn't have all the information about a situation, instead of catastrophizing or jumping to conclusions, they may choose to seek clarity and truly understand their partner's point of view.

- **Trust and respect.** Rather than using clingy or controlling behavior to seek validation or support, secure people are able to give their partners space and time to process their emotions before needing to respond or resolve things.

- **Honest and fair interactions.** Secure people may look at conflict from a more objective perspective, showing empathy and taking the time to truly listen rather than playing the victim role. They may be honest about how they feel, neither minimizing nor magnifying their hurt.

These are the natural results we can expect when we understand and implement the 4 aspects of secure communication. With time and practice, we can begin to shift our anxious communication style to a more secure style and see our relationships expand into mutually fulfilling experiences.

The 4 Aspects Of Secure Communication

When we implement the 4 aspects of secure communication, we can feel empowered to navigate discomfort and conflict in relationships. We can find the confidence to set boundaries, enforce them, and respect the boundaries of others. They include:

1. Active Listening

Anxious communication focuses on trying to gain something from others. When we use passive-aggressive body language, excessively seek validation, or over-exaggerate problems to gain sympathy, we aren't taking time to listen or engage in two-way conversations.

Active listening is a powerful skill that can set us apart in any relationship because it allows us to be fully present and available in a way that nurtures connection. What sets it apart from normal listening is the level of emotional availability displayed. Its success is based on being present enough to form a genuine understanding of others and offer the responses that make them feel seen. We can hear what's really being said beneath our anxious perception.

To improve our listening skills, we can:

- Use a grounding exercise to help us stay present and relaxed in conversation. For example, taking a few deep breaths or centering our awarness on our senses for a moment.

- Resist the urge to think about our own issues, propose our own solutions, or interrupt to redirect attention back to us.

- Use our body language to affirm that we are listening by nodding and smiling when appropriate and maintaining eye contact where comfortable.

- Seek clarity where needed to make sure we understand. For example, we may ask questions like, "So what I'm hearing is that you felt upset when I called you at work? Is that right?"

- Use a tone that is calm and warm, trying not to sound accusatory or judgmental. This is what can take an assertive sentence and turn it into secure communication.

- Respond with questions that encourage more information or reflect our interest. We may use specific language that we've heard in the conversation and leave the questions open-ended. For example, "You said that your father often took you fishing. How did that influence your choice to become a marine biologist?"

2. Empathetic Communication

Our hypervigilance takes a level of empathy that allows us to acutely recognize how others feel. However, it doesn't allow us to take that empathy and use it for good. Instead, we might use it to analyze our partner's emotions so as to avoid conflict, not to support the relationship.

Empathy should serve as a magnetic force that keeps our connections alive and healthy. When we use empathy to communicate our needs, concerns, and insights, it's easier for others to hear us and feel heard in return. Think about the difference between these two sentences:

- Anxious communication: "I get it. You're hurt. But you never listen to me."

- Empathetic communication: "I can see you're hurt. That's not what I intended. I'm hurt, too. When you're ready, let's talk about it?"

Can you see how using empathy to adjust our wording and tone can improve our connections? Empathetic communication is about using our words to show we care and communicating our needs in a more palatable way.

To become more secure, we need to harness our empathetic superpower to deepen our connections. We can use empathy to help us both give and receive the validation needed in satisfying and sustainable relationships. To harness our empathy and communicate securely, we can:

- **Learn to recognize positive intent.** We can use empathy to recognize the intention beneath our partner's delivery. This way, even if they don't say the exact words we want to hear, we can still get the message. For example, if our partners bring us a small thoughtful gift, we can recognize that this means they care for us rather than being concerned about why they didn't say "I love you."

- **Validate others' feelings.** When our partners say, "I'm hurt," we can validate their feelings to make sure they know we truly empathize with them. We may say something like, "I hear that you're hurt. I understand, and I'm here for you," rather than brushing their feelings aside to focus on our own.

- **Validate our own feelings.** Showing others empathy can mean taking responsibility for how we feel rather than blaming or leaving it up to our partners to soothe us every time. For example, during conflict, we might say to ourselves, "I'm hurt, but I'll be okay," as we breathe deeply to regulate ourselves and then respond in a calm tone. (An example of the EGO Technique in practice)

3. Clarity About Our Needs And Boundaries

When we become triggered in relationships, it's often because we have a need that isn't getting met. However, when we are anxiously attached, we may not have the inner security or emotional resilience to state our needs in a clear and reasonable way. We may act out, feel out of control, and become overwhelmed with emotion. This can make the expression of our needs and boundaries feel exhausting for our partners to contend with. They may not understand the intensity we display and choose to withdraw in an effort to cope.

To communicate more securely, we need to get very clear about our needs and boundaries so we can assert them in a way that is easy for others to absorb. Take a moment to go to your Workbook and complete the exercise waiting for you. Use it to reflect on past experiences and write down your most important needs. We will explore boundaries in more depth later in this chapter.

4. Using Concise And Intentional Choice Of Words

Our words have the power to keep our relationships sustainable and expansive. Secure communication involves wording that is approving and concise. Rather than using accusatory language like "you never" or "you always," we can use language like "I feel" or "I think." These are the beginning of "I" statements, an effective communication tool proven to help mediate conflict by avoiding blame and defensiveness.[76]

"I" statements allow us to make assertive statements while retaining all of the responsibility of what we're saying. When we claim our statements in this way, we make it easier for others to hear us without feeling the need to defend themselves. Consider the difference between these anxious Vs. secure communication examples:

- "You always forget to ask me how I'm doing when you get home from work. It's all about you." to "I feel forgotten when you don't ask me how I'm doing after work. How about we take time to reconnect each afternoon?"

- "You're late again! It's obvious you don't care about me." to "I feel disappointed when you're late because it makes me feel like our time together isn't a priority for you."

- "Do you always have to interrupt me? You never listen to what I'm saying!" to "I feel unheard when I'm interrupted.

Could you please wait until I've finished my thoughts before responding with yours?"

- "You never support my dreams. Nobody believes I can do it." to "I feel unsupported when my goals are dismissed. It's important to me to have your encouragement."

- "You're so critical all the time. Why don't you notice everything I do for you?" to "When you criticize me without acknowledging my efforts I feel discouraged to continue putting in work. Positive feedback means a lot to me."

Once we feel comfortable using "I" statements, it's vital that we speak up with confidence. When we speak with uncertainty or fear, we naturally communicate that what we're saying isn't valid or worth hearing. Our statements can sound like part of an emotional outburst rather than a well-thought-out statement that must be taken seriously.

If we are sure and clear about our needs and boundaries, there's nothing to hesitate about. We can use "I" statements to assert them without shame or uncertainty because we know what we deserve.

Secure communication can help us begin to accept that someone worthy of our time will respect our needs and boundaries. We need to advocate for ourselves and accept that if someone is not willing to offer us the same understanding or empathy, then they may not be right for us.

Crossed boundaries are a very serious problem and should never be overlooked for the sake of connection. Part of your secure identity must include a commitment to setting and maintaining healthy boundaries. Before we work on conflict resolution, we need to get very clear on what healthy boundaries are and learn to enforce them without question.

SETTING AND MAINTAINING HEALTHY BOUNDARIES

Boundaries are essential for building secure relationships. They allow us to maintain a healthy level of independence and individuality. Establishing and respecting boundaries creates safe and supportive relationships where both parties can thrive.[77]

It's important to get very clear about our boundaries early on in relationships to ensure that we are with people who are capable and willing to respect them. However, it's also important that our boundaries come from balanced expectations rather than expectations that are unfair or unhealthy.

Although boundaries are meant to be respected at all costs, when they're formed from unhealthy or unrealistic beliefs, we may struggle to find satisfaction in relationships. Boundaries can be controlling and may violate our partner's own boundaries.[78] If we find ourselves repeatedly having our boundaries crossed and ending relationships with good people, it may be that our boundaries are unreasonable.

Examples of unhealthy boundaries may include:

- Needing constant contact with our partners, even when we know they are at important events or spending time with family.

- Not allowing our partners to attend social or family events without us, even if we're too busy to attend.

- Insisting on access to our partner's social media accounts and messaging apps to monitor and control their social engagement.

- Dictating what our partners can wear, which hobbies we find acceptable for them to enjoy, and other personal aspects of who they are.

- Expecting our partners to dedicate all their free time to the relationship, even if that means neglecting their friendships, family relationships, or physical health.

Boundaries must respect the autonomy and characteristics of others.[79] We can't expect people to change who they are to be with us. However, that doesn't mean we can't enforce boundaries that encourage our partners to grow as people. For example, if we enforce a boundary like "Intimacy is important to me, I need a partner who can talk openly about their emotions." we may encourage an emotionally unavailable partner to develop more emotional intelligence.

Just as we did with our needs, to enforce our boundaries effectively, we need to get very clear on what they are. Take time to reflect carefully on your current boundaries and consider which ones may not be healthy. If your boundaries have been ineffective, be sure to contemplate what may be missing. Think about adding boundaries that can support secure relationships like:

- Enough personal time and space.

- Respecting each other's privacy.

- Commitment to clear and honest communication.

- Mutual appreciation and respect for each other.

- Financial independence and transparency regarding mutual investments.

- Balanced and considerate time management, ensuring ample time together.

- A consistent conflict resolution approach where both parties feel they can regulate.[80]

When we're caught up in a new relationship or conflict, we may begin to feel our boundaries dissolve under the emotional intensity. Having them written down can give us a resource to refer back to during these times so we can ensure we are staying safe and satisfied in relationships. In your Workbook, take a moment to reflect and write down your boundaries with the help of the prompts available. Once we're clear about what our boundaries are, we can practice enforcing them with a secure communication style.

Boundaries require clear and concise language with an empathetic tone to make sure they are heard and respected easily. We want to avoid any antagonistic or critical language while reflecting the seriousness of having our boundaries respected. We might communicate our boundaries with reassuring phrases, "I" statements, and empathy without retracting from their clarity.[81] For example,

- "I trust you. Let's agree to keep our phones private unless we choose to share something?"

- "My privacy is important to me. Can we agree to knock before entering each other's space?"

- "I feel shut down when I hear shouting. When we disagree, can we talk about it openly and calmly? And if we need space to cool down, let's respectfully take a moment of alone time before we resolve things."

- "Physical closeness makes me feel secure in our relationship. However, let's commit to checking and making sure the other person feels receptive before engaging intimately."

- "It's important to me that I feel safe sharing my feelings without shame or judgment. How can we create a space where we both feel comfortable listening and sharing?"

In secure relationships, it's important to find a balance between enforcing our own boundaries and respecting the boundaries of others. Having firm but reasonable boundaries can form part of our secure foundation, allowing us to manage the ups and downs of relationships with self-confidence.

Anxious attachment may make us prone to bending our boundaries. However, it's vital that we're clear about what crossed boundaries mean for the relationship. The point of setting and enforcing a boundary is knowing what actions or level of neglect we are willing to withstand before we end the relationship. Beneath each boundary we set there must be a prerequisite of "If you don't respect my boundaries, I can't stay in the relationship." It's that simple.

Enforcing boundaries can be uncomfortable, as we risk rejection, judgment, or conflict. Have you ever had to tell someone you love they've crossed a boundary? It's a difficult conversation to have, especially if we don't approach it with sufficient care. Good people don't like to know they've hurt someone, but our delivery can make all the difference.

DIFFICULT CONVERSATIONS AND CONFLICT RESOLUTION

If we have been clear about our boundaries, needs, and emotions, it's up to our partners to meet us in the middle. Part of the importance of being secure means standing our ground and making space for our partners to step up. We don't need to chase, overcompensate, or reduce ourselves. We can show up, do our part, and accept that our partners may or may not do theirs.

We've made so much progress stepping out of The Self-Sabotage Cycle, but conflict is a common trigger that could pull us back in if we don't handle it well. To continue to be clear about what we need in our relationships, we may have to initiate uncomfortable conversations. However, we can adopt a new approach to conflict. It's possible to use secure communication to help navigate conflict in new and productive ways.

In Chapter 3, we spoke about triggers and how they create the negative thoughts, emotions, and protest behaviors common in anxious attachment. Now that we've reflected on our needs and boundaries and how we tend to shrink them for the comfort of others, we need to do things differently.

Healthy conflict resolution involves applying what we've learned throughout the book to approach conflict more securely.

Healthy Conflict Resolution

Conflict requires emotional intelligence and self-care for us to navigate it effectively. We need to be able to manage ourselves and positively influence the outcome for both parties. Managing conflict is not about winning, it's about connecting.[82]

When we come into conflict with someone we care about, it's easy to feel disconnected from them, as if we are their opponent in a fight. Healthy conflict resolution means navigating conflict as a team. There are 5 steps we can take to do this effectively, including:

Step 1: The EGO Technique For Two

We already have a host of strategies we can use to support ourselves in emotionally intense situations. The EGO Technique is a great first response to conflict as it helps us regain a sense of control. To apply the EGO Technique *For Two*, we can:

- Encounter our triggers while also recognizing that our partners may be triggered as well.
- Ground ourselves, which may prevent the conflict from escalating.
- Own our true needs and be receptive to hearing our partner's needs as well.

Step 2: Pause And Address The Unmet Emotional Needs

Rather than evading the real problem, we can address our unmet needs early on and resolve the conflict at its core. If the conflict extends over a period, we can support ourselves by using other regulation tactics, like the Calm Coping Technique, to soothe our emotions. Even if it's a need we can't expect our partners to meet right away, we can make progress by affirming the need. For example, if our unmet need is:

- **Feelings of safety:** We can move to a place of physical safety or calmly request that our partners stop their behaviors that are making us feel unsafe.

- **Emotional validation:** We can validate our own emotions by acknowledging them and reminding ourselves that how we feel makes sense. We might find a constructive way to soothe our emotions, like taking a walk with our partners or taking a short time-out.

- **Physical affection:** We can soothe ourselves with loving touch, such as a self-hug, gently rubbing our arms or legs, or any other soothing touch we can offer ourselves during conflict.

Addressing our unmet needs early on can help us feel regulated enough to resolve conflict more effectively. It allows us to find enough calm and understanding in our own experience to move forward from a supportive frame of mind. We can then take steps to understand our partners and reach a mutual resolution.

Step 3: Say Less And Do More

Everyone will have unique needs during conflict, but sometimes, saying less and doing more is the easiest way forward. We can find ways to *show* our partners we care to help bring their guard down. That means becoming an attractive and loving force rather than a repelling one. It's difficult to be in conflict with someone when we're on the same side. To shift our energy and invite our partners to reconnect, we can:

- **Soften our body language.** We may drop our hands, unclench our jaws, relax our facial expressions, drop our shoulders, and allow our entire demeanor to appear less threatening.

- **Lower our tone of voice.** Rather than talking with a loud, harsh tone, we can purposefully begin to speak in a loving tone of voice.

- **Offer physical touch.** If our partners enjoy physical touch, touch is one of the most powerful ways to connect with someone. We may gently take their hand, invite them in for a hug, or allow our feet to touch theirs under the table.

- **Complete a random act of kindness.** Sometimes, doing something kind, no matter how small is enough to open up a gentle line of communication. For example, we could bring our partner a cup of tea, a snack, or help them with a task.

Whatever small or subtle way we choose to reconnect with our partners, it's important that we start to see each other as equals and not as opponents.

Step 4: Adjust For Vulnerability And Listen

If we want to start a line of healthy communication during conflict, we can't expect our partners to be vulnerable without creating a safe space for them to open up. Once we've softened our energy to attract rather than repel, we can lead by example and offer vulnerability first.

We should use "I" statements to calmly assert how we feel, followed by active listening. If our partners are quiet, we can gently ask them how they feel with an open-ended question like "I see you're hurting. Can you help me understand how you feel?" And if our partners try to open up, we can simply listen with empathy, remove any distractions, and be prepared to respond with compassion.

Step 5: Communicate Securely With Compassion

Conflict can be extremely uncomfortable, but it's important that we don't try to rush through it or escape it. Working through conflict thoroughly and with compassion will help reduce the chances of it reoccurring. Compassionate, secure communication allows us to resolve conflict and reach an agreement that feels satisfying for both parties. We can work as a team to find a solution using language that is affirming, understanding, and assertive.

Secure conflict resolution might include statements like:

- "We're both upset, and that's okay. Let's pause for 10 minutes to cool down and then talk this through." rather than "Calm down! I'm hurt too, you know."

- "I said things that were hurtful, and I'm sorry. I let my anger get the better of me." rather than, "You're the one who started all this. Why should I say sorry?"

- "We both care about each other. Let's focus on finding a solution together that works for both of us." rather than, "Don't you get that I care about you? I'm trying to fix this. What are you doing?"

- "Can I hold your hand while we talk? I care about you, and I want us to work together to resolve this." rather than "Don't touch me! I haven't forgiven you."

- "Dinners almost ready. Why don't we talk about what happened earlier? I want to hear your side of things." rather than ignoring the argument and eating dinner in front of the TV.

CONCLUSION

A secure communication style can be enough to keep us out of The Self-Sabotage Cycle as we communicate our boundaries and manage conflict in fair and effective ways. We can combine all the cycle-breaking tools we've learned so far and navigate some of the toughest times in our relationships with more inner security, compassion, and emotional intelligence. We can create far better outcomes than we may be used to.

With practice, we can use our communication style to become more vulnerable and create an environment where others feel safe to be vulnerable with us. Vulnerability is a fundamental link to building trust and intimacy in relationships.

That leads us to Chapter 8, where we will explore how vulnerability, trust, and intimacy work to develop deep, authentic connections.

8

DEEP TRUST, INTIMACY, AND VULNERABILITY

Techniques To Create Closeness

*"He who does not trust enough,
Will not be trusted."*

– Lao Tzu

THE FOUNDATION OF SECURE AND FULFILLING RELATIONSHIPS

In fulfilling relationships, the cycle of trust, vulnerability, and intimacy is free-flowing. We rarely question whether we can trust our partners, we feel safe being vulnerable with them, and intimacy is a natural result. When we spend time nurturing one of the three elements of this cycle, we create safety for the others to exist and thrive. However, it all starts with trust.

Trust is the foundation of secure, fulfilling relationships. It forms the basis for safety and security. Without trust, we don't feel safe enough to open up and be vulnerable. And if we can't let our guard down to be vulnerable, intimacy might feel forced and uncomfortable.

Anxious attachment can fill our minds with enough doubt and fear to disturb our trust in others.[83] We may rarely feel safe enough to be fully honest and true to ourselves. Although intimacy is something we desire deeply, our lack of inner security may make intimate interactions feel tense and anxiety-provoking. We may analyze every word or action and question our partner's sincerity. Even if our relationship is otherwise healthy, it may still feel like something is wrong when nothing truly is.

 My relationship used to reach the point of breakdown every couple of months because of my anxious attachment. But my newfound ability to trust, be vulnerable, and feel comfortable building our intimate connection has gifted me with a love I never thought I could muster – a secure love. In this chapter, we will address each aspect of the trust, vulnerability, and intimacy cycle and explore the many ways you can actively change your core mistrust in others so you can experience the full depth of a loving relationship as I did.

TRUST

Trust forms the foundation of our relationships and can dictate their success.[84] A strong sense of trust in someone allows us to feel safe. Our minds no longer need to stay on high alert and we can focus on more important things like forming a deeper emotional connection. But to understand trust and ensure we nurture it in all our relationships, we have to understand what it entails.

The 5 Components Of Trust

When our trust is something we can flip on and off like a switch, it isn't coming from a genuine sense of trust for someone. To harbor authentic trust in any relationship, we have to consider the 5 Components Of Trust and how we may fall short of them when we exhibit our anxious attachment.[85]

1. Honesty

Honesty is about telling the truth and being transparent in our actions. It builds trust because when we are honest in what we say and do, others feel able to believe in our good nature. In a secure relationship, both parties can share openly and honestly with no need for suspicion or avoidance of full disclosure.

In anxious attachment, we may not feel comfortable sharing our honest feelings or being honest about who we are. Our fear of rejection or abandonment can keep us from telling the truth and being trustworthy. We may also frequently doubt the honesty of others as we may hold misbeliefs about their intentions and feel suspicious or hypervigilant about their flaws.

2. Reliability

In a secure relationship, both parties can be mutually reliant on each other, fostering trust and connection. This can mean doing the things we say we're going to do, following through on promises, and being positively predictable in our behavior.

Anxious attachment can cause us to behave unpredictably. Our partners may not feel certain about how we will respond in various situations as we may respond emotionally sometimes and withdraw at other times, creating anxiety and mistrust in the relationships.

3. Emotional Safety

Secure relationships are emotionally safe relationships. Emotional safety is the feeling of safety to show and express our true emotions. We can share our innermost thoughts, desires, and feelings without the fear of rejection or judgment. We know that our partners will respond with compassion and an understanding of who we are.

In anxious attachment, we may not feel safe expressing our emotions as we may not have the tools to manage our emotions enough to express them safely. Unsafe emotional expression damages emotional safety for us and for our partners, as our expression may cause them to respond in ways that further our anxiety.

4. Support

Support in relationships is a matter of being present and emotionally available in the face of challenges. Consistent support builds trust and a feeling of partnership that makes life's struggles and celebrations worthwhile. Mutual support strengthens a relationship's resilience and forms a valuable part of a strong emotional connection.

When we're anxiously attached, we may perceive our partner's support as dwindling and feel unsupported even when our partners are trying their best to be supportive. We may hold back from asking for support or expressing our needs for fear of being a burden. Alternatively, we may excessively ask for support or reassurance, leaving our partners feeling drained.

5. Respect

Respect is an essential element of trust because it only takes one moment of disrespect to damage it. In secure relationships, both parties equally respect each other's boundaries, needs, and autonomy. Consistent respect keeps trust intact and offers us the security we need regarding how our partners feel about us. Mutual respect lays a foundation for appreciation and a sense of equality that can make us feel understood and valued.

The relationship dynamics created by anxious attachment can produce ample opportunities for feelings of disrespect. Our relationships may harbor many misunderstandings, hurtful behavior, and a disregard for our partner's needs as we bombard them with requests and accusations. Our over-dependence can be perceived as disrespectful and a breach of trust each time we feel insecure enough to act out or withdraw.

Now that we've discussed the 5 components of trust and all the ways we may sabotage it, let's talk about how to rebuild and maintain trust effectively.

Rebuilding And Maintaining Trust

Building trust is a matter of implementing and maintaining honesty, reliability, emotional safety, support, and respect in our relationships. As we continue, keep in mind that trust can take time to build or restore. We need to stay consistent and authentic with our approach and be patient with the outcome.[86] Building or rebuilding trust will require:

1. Honesty

To maintain honesty in relationships and establish trust, we can:

- Commit to transparency and open communication.
- Make a habit of sharing our thoughts, desires, and emotions even when it's difficult.
- Avoid white lies and exclusion of facts that may cause conflict later on.
- Own up to our mistakes and be willing to talk them through honestly.

2. Reliability

With a long-term approach, we can prove our reliability by:

- Consistently following through with any commitment or promise.

- Prioritizing quick and honest communication about any authentic changes or obstacles that may stop us from fulfilling our promises.

- Take any opportunity to be dependable, showing up in our relationships effectively. For example, ensuring we attend important events or offer to help with tasks.

- Maintaining a level of predictability in our actions and behavior. For example, responding to conflict in a calm and consistent way.

3. Emotional Safety

Emotional safety is something we may know we need but struggle to replicate. Intense emotions are a major part of anxious attachment. We may feel as though we need emotional safety to respond better in conflict, but the two are interchangeably effective. We can create emotional safety in our relationships by:

- Effectively managing our emotions using the secure techniques we developed in Chapter 5.

- Listening actively and empathetically, making sure to respond with compassion.

- Recognizing and validating others' experiences and feelings.

- Apologizing for any emotional harm or neglect we're responsible for.

4. Support

To bypass our anxious attachment and nurture a supportive dynamic between us and others, we can:

- Be present and available, making sure to offer encouragement and assistance if needed.

- Maintain emotional availability during difficult times, showing empathy and understanding.

- Celebrate others' success and give them the recognition they deserve.

- Asking others what kind of support they need and making a genuine effort to provide it.

- Recognize others' attempts to support us and acknowledge their efforts.

- Assert our needs for support using a secure communication style and giving others a fair chance to show up for us.

Support is a great example of the say less, do more step when practicing secure communication, as it allows us to *show* others how much we care. When rebuilding broken trust, it's important that we acknowledge where we went wrong and continue to show up in the relationship.

5. Respect

The most important time to exercise respect for others is during conflict. To maintain trust, we must maintain respect in our relationships throughout the good and bad times. We can:

- Honor each other's boundaries and individuality.
- Accept and encourage each other's autonomy.
- Value and appreciate others' needs, opinions, and differences.
- Commit to respectful communication even during disagreements.
- Work on the first 4 components of trust in an authentic and consistent way.

Anxious attachment may cause breaches in trust to affirm false beliefs about others and relationships. However, to build inner security and cope with conflict fairly, we must remember that people are only human. Anyone can make a mistake. How they handle their mistake is more important when trying to discern how forgiving we're willing to be.

To ensure others are worthy of our trust, we can look out for the 5 components of trust in their behavior. We can hold them accountable for mistakes or flaws and give them ample opportunities to show up for us. When both partners commit to trust, relationships can find security with ease.[87]

Once trust is established, vulnerability becomes a natural skill that can grow alongside it. Even so, it's important to practice and become more comfortable with vulnerability to nurture deeper connections. I'd like to share a technique known as the GROW Technique that helped me bypass my fear of vulnerability. This is another essential tool for building secure love.

VULNERABILITY

When we are anxiously attached, fear is in the driver's seat. We allow it to control what we do, what we say, and the choices we make. But when fear is driving, our authenticity takes a backseat. We don't show up in relationships honestly, we're unpredictable, and our focus is often on staying safe rather than being genuine. Fear diverts the 5 components of trust, making it difficult to:

- Trust others; and
- Be trustworthy.

To overcome anxious attachment, we need to overcome fear. We need to feel the fear and make new choices despite it. We need to embrace vulnerability and become okay with being a little at risk. Seeking safety in relationships is not a sustainable strategy. Relationships bring challenges and conflict which we may perceive as threatening. Safety seeking is our anxious attachment, our fear taking the wheel.

To bypass fear and gain a powerful sense of security in relationships, we need to prioritize vulnerability over safety. Rather than working so hard to control our relationships in an effort to feel comfortable all the time, we need to seek discomfort in the pursuit of deeper connection.

Vulnerability is an excellent desensitizing tool for expanding our comfort zones and relinquishing control in anxious attachment. As you go through The GROW Technique, consider relationships a playground where you get to know yourself so others can get to know you, too.

Use the LearnWell Community to practice what you learn.

Being Vulnerable Using The GROW Technique

Vulnerability is an essential part of the Trust, Vulnerability, and Intimacy cycle. Without it, we hold ourselves back from having beautiful, trusting, and emotionally intimate relationships. In anxious attachment, our fears may impact vulnerability by:

- Making us doubt whether our true selves are worthy of love and intimacy.
- Causing uncertainty about our partner's trustworthiness.
- Excessively seeking reassurance and vulnerability from others without feeling secure enough to be vulnerable in return.
- Sabotaging vulnerable moments with negative thinking, overwhelming emotions, and protest behaviors.

To open up and practice vulnerability, we can apply **The GROW Technique**, where we take practical steps to overcome fear and let go of control. We can:

Get Quiet

When our minds are full of cognitive distortions, we may overlook others' vulnerability. We may be distracted by our thoughts, doubts, or emotions and miss valuable opportunities to connect deeply. To practice vulnerability, we can start by getting quiet in our minds and bodies. We need to become receptive to moments of vulnerability in others or opportunities to take the first step toward vulnerability.

Recognize The Block

When we're anxiously attached, there are a host of blocks that can hinder our vulnerability. They may be thoughts, emotions, beliefs, or fears that make us feel unsafe to open up. To move forward, we need to identify our blocks and understand where they originate. With the work we've done throughout Parts 2 and 3, finding the origin of our blocks may come easy. However, some vulnerability blocks may include:

- Fear of rejection, abandonment, or conflict.
- Negative thinking like "What if they judge me?" or "What if they don't love me anymore if I share this?"
- Intense emotions like anxiety, anger, or self-deprecating sadness that may detract from our ability to speak securely.

Simply recognizing the block may be enough to loosen it and give us the strength to open up. However, there's no rush to push our blocks aside and jump into vulnerability before we're ready.

Open Up Slowly

It's important that we approach vulnerability from a stable and gradual place to ensure our intentions behind sharing are genuine and fair rather than anxious or desperate for connection. If genuine vulnerability is difficult for us, we can use the concept of gradual exposure to ease into vulnerability at a rate that feels nurturing to us and others.

Welcome Discomfort

Bypassing the fears and blocks standing in our way of vulnerability will naturally cause some or even a lot of discomfort. Vulnerability can leave us feeling exposed to rejection or judgment, especially if we are the first to open up in a relationship. Building up the courage and confidence to be vulnerable with others means welcoming discomfort in the pursuit of deeper connections.

Implementing the GROW Technique can help us practice vulnerability without leaving us exposed or isolated. It allows us to draw others in with an openness that encourages vulnerability in return. If we can resist the urge to anxiously share in an attempt to speed up connection or withdraw when we are met with rejection, then we place ourselves in a good position to truly connect.

With patience and a focus on growing our vulnerability in a well-intentioned way, we can deepen our connections enough to invite more intimate interactions. Intimacy is one of the most powerful ways to build a secure connection. However, there is a difference between emotional and physical intimacy. Which one are you more familiar with? They're both vital to your journey, but balancing them must be your priority.

INTIMACY

Anxious attachment can create confusion around intimacy, potentially causing a misunderstanding about the difference between emotional and physical intimacy. We may become too attached too quickly if we experience physical intimacy with someone, or we may push to progress intimacy before others feel comfortable.[88]

Our fear of abandonment may also make us prone to accepting intimate interactions when we're not ready or comfortable. Poorly reciprocated or forced intimacy can not only slow connection but can be deeply damaging.[89]

It's important that we understand the power of intimacy and how to cultivate both emotional and physical intimacy in appropriate and loving ways. To start, lets get clear on the difference:

- **Emotional intimacy:** Involves sharing thoughts, feelings, and experiences on a deeply emotional level. It requires a level of trust and vulnerability that allows us to feel comfortable being open and honest while helping others feel seen and heard.

- **Physical intimacy:** Involves physical closeness and touch, which can include hugs, hand holding, kissing, and sexual activities. It requires a level of trust and vulnerability that allows us to express affection and love through physical contact or proximity. Physical intimacy is not exclusive to romantic relationships provided that proper boundaries are in place. For example, reserving sexual activities for romantic relationships only.

Physical and emotional intimacy can merge in many interactions. For example, deep emotional conversations that lead to kissing or a vulnerable moment with a friend that causes us to reach out and take their hand. The level of intimacy we display in relationships is generally what separates relationships into their various categories, ie., friendships, romantic relationships, and family.

To nurture secure and loving relationships, it's important to cultivate intimacy in ways that feel appropriate and comfortable for both parties. Each relationship will have a unique expression of intimacy. What's important is that we don't leave it out in our pursuit of secure relationships. When we're anxiously attached, we may push the boundaries of intimacy before a relationship has matured. We may force intimacy on others by demanding interactions they are not comfortable with.[90] We may sabotage intimacy by:

- **Using the need for reassurance as a way to force intimacy.** For example, requesting others say things like "I love you" when they're not ready.

- **Oversharing personal details about our lives, needs, or desires too soon.** For example, talking about our desire to get married or have children on a first date.

- **Emotional or physical clinginess.** For example, we may request our partners spend all their free time with us or excessively ask for physical intimacy without allowing it to occur naturally. We may also ask for kisses without gauging our partner's receptivity rather than creating loving circumstances where kissing is a natural result.

- **Violating our partners privacy.** For example, wanting to read our partners texts when we feel jealous may sabotage our partner's trust, creating a resistance to intimacy.

- **Pushing for physically intimate interactions.** For example, pressuring our partners into levels of physical intimacy they're not ready for, which can lead to discomfort, broken trust, and feelings of violation.

To build strong, secure relationships with deep emotional intimacy, we need to transition from our anxious behavior and practice behaving in new ways that naturally lead to intimacy.

While physical intimacy is an important part of deepening connections, we should focus on creating a safe environment for others and building the emotional intimacy needed for positive physical touch. Now, let's get into the practical ways we can build intimacy in our relationships.

Practical Ways Of Building Intimacy

Building intimacy isn't a difficult task. It can be one of the most fun and rewarding steps you take along your journey toward more secure relationships. Once you're open to it, simply put yourself and others in situations where intimacy feels natural. Here are some ideas:

Start With Good Conversations

Creating a safe space for emotional openness is crucial in any relationship. We want to be someone others feel safe enough around to let their guard down. Good conversations are open and honest. They provide a space for both parties to freely express themselves and feel heard.

We can exercise our secure communication skills and actively make it okay to discuss emotions and thoughts with us. If we often respond in an emotionally balanced and empathetic way, others will trust that we are a safe person with whom to create a foundation for intimate interactions.

Bond Through Shared Activities And Adventures

Building a strong emotional connection can be as simple as getting out of the house and sharing experiences together. Shared activities and adventures have a powerful bonding potential without needing to put too much pressure on the outcome. We can build emotional intimacy while having fun together in memorable ways. Depending on our interests and capabilities, some excellent activities that promote emotional intimacy and sometimes physical intimacy include:

- Hiking
- Camping
- Board games
- Going for a run
- Craft classes
- Trying new things
- Cooking a meal
- Volunteering
- Dancing
- Traveling

When choosing bonding activities, we should always consider what each person is comfortable with. Activities that are positively challenging, fun, or relaxing are all great options when all parties included are up for it.

Prioritize Quality Time And Presence

Time spent in the same vicinity and quality time have two very different effects on a relationship. One is emotionally intimate, building trust and creating space for vulnerability, while the other isn't. Quality time is intentional time spent with someone where we make an effort to be emotionally present and open to connection. For example, sitting in front of the TV is generally not seen as quality time. However, choosing a good movie, setting up a snack board, and intentionally snuggling up in front of the TV together can be an emotional bonding experience.

To turn time spent together into quality time that improves emotional intimacy, we can:

- Remove distractions like cellphones or certain lighting.
- Make an effort to engage and listen with secure communication.
- Schedule regular quality time with the people we care about.
- Choose activities that satisfy a mutual interest.
- Take turns supporting each other's goals and interests.
- Put our personal worries, problems, and obligations aside.

Presence and quality time is an important part of any relationship. To keep our relationships emotionally healthy, we must prioritize intentionally showing up in our relationships without the distraction of technology or personal problems. We can use quality time as breathing room from our anxieties about the relationship. Try to be present and allow the experience to put your mind at ease.

Create Meaningful Rituals And Traditions

Meaningful rituals and traditions are a powerful way to foster long-term emotional intimacy and connection. They give us something to look forward to in relationships. As we create and stick to the rituals and traditions that form part of our relationships, we create a lasting legacy of positive emotions and bonding. Rituals and traditions don't have to form part of any well-established holiday or stereotype. We can create them to suit our unique connections and build them into something we genuinely anticipate. To create rituals and traditions that mean the most, we can:

- Identify what matters most in the relationship.
- Start small and stay consistent.
- Make them personal.
- Be flexible to change.

We can use rituals and traditions as a part of everyday life to add a sense of exciting sameness, comfort, and celebration to the mundanities of life. Our traditions and rituals can also add a personal element to popular celebrations or holidays like birthdays or major public holidays. With our growing sense of security, we can see these traditions and rituals as reassurance that our relationships are healthy.

Intimacy is an effective tool for deep emotional connections. It is the natural outcome of quality time with others and can lead to great relationship security. However, we can also use trust, vulnerability, and intimacy to reinforce each other. As we work on building one, the other two will improve as well.

Unlearning my anxious attachment and saving my relationship wasn't easy. Trust is the most important aspect of a secure, long-lasting relationship, but building it was the most difficult part of my journey. It started with a brief moment of vulnerability and led to a quickly expanding well of experiences that built my relationship up from the ground up.

Sometimes, all it takes to move past broken trust or fears is an open mind and one good experience. Once you have that one good experience, whether it's in trust, vulnerability, or intimacy, roll with it. Make room for more, and expand.

CONCLUSION: THE REWARDS OF DEEP, AUTHENTIC CONNECTION

Trust, vulnerability, and intimacy are 3 key components of a secure relationship. They foster deep, authentic connections where we can freely express our authentic selves. They also allow us to create an environment where others feel safe to be authentic in return.

When we cultivate these 3 essential elements of secure relationships, anxious attachment no longer has room to keep us in The Self-Sabotage Cycle. Consider this

- Our trust can build into a powerful force of security that keeps negative thoughts at bay.
- Our vulnerability gives us enough opportunities for a deep, satisfying sense of connection; and

- The level of intimacy we experience can soothe our wounds at their core.

With these ideas, you're building a strong foundation for your relationships and beginning to exhibit the attributes of secure attachment. Continue that in your Workbook, where you'll find an exercise that guides you through a plan for developing trust, vulnerability, and intimacy in your own relationship or preparing for it in future relationships. Do this while these ideas are fresh in your mind.

Having built this foundation, we can consistently approach our connections from a sense of wholeness within ourselves that prepares us for whole and beautiful relationships. We can continue to practice all that we've learned and fortify our sense of secure attachment. That's what Part 4 is all about. When you're ready, let's move through the final chapter of this book and ensure the future of your relationships is something you look forward to.

PART 4

STRATEGIES FOR LASTING CHANGE

9

SECURE, IN LOVE, NOW, AND FOREVER

Making Secure Feel Normal

"Love is the flower you've got to let grow."
– John Lennon

THE JOURNEY FROM ANXIOUS TO SECURE ATTACHMENT

The first time I felt secure it was in the midst of things going wrong. My partner had taken a job in a city almost a thousand miles away, and we were already a couple of months into our long-distance arrangement. Although temporary, the time apart triggered my anxious attachment in every way possible. I was becoming hysterical and couldn't do anything but ruminate on the situation. I knew I was anxiously attached and had already done a lot of healing, but these were new waters for me to navigate, and I was drowning.

The progress I had made started to feel redundant. My symptoms felt intense, and my behavior started causing problems again. Every time my partner would call, I'd be asking for reassurance or giving him trouble about not talking to me enough. Eventually, the calls got shorter, less frequent, and less connected. Our relationship hung in the air as we both waited for something to give.

After a couple of grueling arguments, I started to reevaluate. I paused and took the time to face the reality of the situation. My anxiety had reached a boiling point, and I couldn't endure the intensity any longer. And that was when it happened. All the progress I'd made before this major setback came together, and I felt a sense of something new. I felt a sense of detachment that, while jarring at first, soon settled into acceptance. I took a deep breath and let go of the part of me still clinging to the success of this relationship. It wasn't me giving up, rather, surrendering.

For someone who was anxiously attached, some healthy detachment was what I needed to teach me how to let go. Rather than trying to force an outcome that met my rigid expectations, I surrendered to the natural flow of the relationship – even if that meant losing it. It was painful at first, and I felt abandoned on a very deep level. But over time, as my partner and I stayed consistent with daily check-ins and an agreement of quality time from a distance, I began to understand the nature of a secure relationship. Like an elastic band recoiling into comfort, letting go eased the tension and gave my partner the space to bounce back to me.

Anxious attachment creates tension, force, and damage that strains our relationships. The more we push for the outcome we want, the more we stretch the rubber band. However, when we can surrender and accept that what's meant for us will stay with us, we stop pulling. We can let go, put our energy into becoming someone others don't want to lose, and watch as our relationships come back together.

Of course, it's not as simple as letting go and retracting all effort. We still have to nurture our relationships and show up for our partners. But because anxious attachment tends to involve overexertion of effort in the wrong places, becoming secure may mean learning to slow down and do less. It's a matter of using our energy in wiser ways and directing much of it to becoming more secure in ourselves so we can be more secure around others.

Secure connections are built on a foundation of two secure people. If we want secure relationships, we have to:

- Become secure people
- Choose secure partners

Secure people are not unicorns in our society. They are simply people with the emotional intelligence to manage their own thoughts, emotions, and behaviors well and who believe they deserve to be treated well by others. They have a healthy sense of self-compassion and love, and they ensure that their needs and boundaries are met in relationships, even at the expense of losing people who aren't willing to match up. Secure people are trustworthy, able to be vulnerable, and easy to feel close to. They know who they are, and they aren't afraid of authenticity.

Throughout Chapters 1 - 8, we've been on a journey of self-discovery that has led us to a very important point. We've been gently unraveling our anxious conditioning, and we've made significant progress toward inner security. With time, practice, and the right application of our new skills we can transition to secure attachment and experience connections that grow and bounce back from conflict with far less anxiety. In this Chapter, we will bring all our expanding traits and skills together so we can become secure people and build the secure relationships we've envisioned for so long.

CULTIVATING SECURE ATTACHMENT BEHAVIORS

Our growth and behavior is our responsibility. We have so much more control over who we want to be than we may realize. Even if we sustain wounds, the way we choose to address our wounds and live our lives can mean the difference between anxious and secure attachment. Secure attachment doesn't mean we don't have flaws or challenges in relationships, but rather that we have the tools to manage difficulties without damaging our relationships. To cultivate secure attachment, we can implement the secure behaviors we've learned, which include:

- Practicing self-compassion through self-kindness, common humanity, and mindfulness.
- Understanding and managing our emotions with emotional resilience and self-awareness.
- Developing our interpersonal skills so we can show empathy and listen actively.
- Building a strong sense of self and finding the self-confidence to be authentic.
- Getting clear on our needs, values, beliefs, and boundaries and sharing them assertively.
- Exercising secure communication so we can be both assertive and empathetic.
- Coping with conflict using secure conflict intervention techniques.
- Prioritizing deeper connections by being trustworthy, vulnerable, and intimate.

Each of these secure behaviors is essential to cultivating secure relationship dynamics.[91] We can use our energy wisely by focusing on ourselves and showing up in relationships more securely. We stop trying to control the outcome of our relationships and instead create a safe and loving environment for others to magnetize toward us. Remember, we already have value. Becoming more secure is about giving that value the space and care to grow and be seen without the fog of anxious attachment.

Assessing Our Current Relationship Dynamics

As we implement secure behaviors, we need to assess our current relationship dynamics for signs and symptoms of anxious attachment. Recognizing our current patterns, including our relationship strengths and weaknesses, can equip us with the insights needed to move forward more effectively. We can share what we've noticed with our partners and work together to focus our efforts where they're needed most. Consider the signs and symptoms of anxious attachment covered in Chapter 1. You can find a simplified list in your Workbook.

With these patterns in mind, reflect on your current relationship. In your Workbook, tick off the patterns you've noticed and write down how you and your partner might be able to improve the dynamic. Use the list of secure behaviors as inspiration. This exercise may serve as a great resource, reminding you of the progress you make.

Once we have reflected on our relationship dynamics and how we might improve on them, we need to involve our partners in this process. Using secure communication skills, we can gauge our partners' receptivity and choose a time that suits both parties. When we bring up our insights, we can use "I" statements to assert our thoughts and opinions while respectfully understanding that our partners may feel differently. We may say things like:

- "This relationship is important to me and I care about you a lot. However, I've noticed that when we argue, I feel out of control, and you seem to shut down. Can we discuss ways we can come together and soothe each other in those moments?"

- "How are you? Do you feel up for some quality time tonight? I've got some ideas I'd like to run by you that might be great for connecting."

- "I've been reading up on attachment styles and it's been enlightening. After much self-reflection, I believe I am anxiously attached, and it's impacting our relationship in ways I'd like to improve. Are you free to hear more?"

We may need to adjust our approach to initiating a conversation about relationship insights and improvements based on our partners' receptivity, availability, and the current depth of the connection. After years of anxious attachment, our relationships are likely to be strained, and initiating conversations about the relationship may put our partners on guard for conflict.

For the best outcome, it's important that we meet our partners where they are and take things as slow as we need to. We must also stay receptive to their insights in return to ensure they play an active role in healing the relationship. If we are trying to rebuild after a period of hurt, we can keep our reflections to ourselves until we have reconciled any immediate issues.

Rebuilding Trust And Repairing Ruptures With The CARE Repair Technique

Secure relationships can still experience arguments. The difference is in the destructiveness of the conflict. Whether we're healing a relationship damaged by anxious attachment or choosing to cope with future conflict in a more secure way, we can use **The CARE Repair Technique** to combine everything we've learned about healthy conflict resolution.

When things go wrong in our relationships, we may need to rebuild trust and repair our connections. The CARE Repair Technique allows us to take active steps towards real repair. We must apply each step with a secure approach that builds the relationship up long-term rather than using it to simply get through the argument and get things back to normal.

C - *Communicate Openly, Assertively, And Empathetically*

In secure relationships, it's important that we don't withhold information from our partners for fear of upsetting them, being judged, or feeling abandoned. We need to communicate openly, assertively share our needs and thoughts, and use an empathetic tone to help our words feel more digestible. We can use "I" statements to help us choose words that clearly communicate how we feel while taking full responsibility for our experience of things.

A - *Acknowledge And Validate Each Other's Emotions*

As we continue to discuss things, we should make a point of acknowledging our partners' emotions and validating their experiences. This way, we can ensure our partners feel heard and give them the opportunity to acknowledge and validate our emotions in return.

It's also important to verbally acknowledge each other's experiences to ensure an accurate understanding. For example, we may say, "I can see that you're hurt. I'm presuming it's because I raised my voice at you. Is that right?" As long as we use a calm and empathetic tone of voice, our partners should be receptive to having their emotions validated.

R - Repair Our Connection With A Sincere Apology

We can offer a sincere apology at any stage during this strategy. Whenever we feel genuinely apologetic about our actions or our partner's hurt, we can speak up and repair the connection with a sincere apology. However, we should not go through the strategy without apologizing.

Regardless of what the conflict or relationship breakdown was about, both parties always have a role to play, even if that is simply engaging negatively in conflict initiated by the other. Apologies are a way for us to actively take responsibility for our side of things and to show that we care. A good apology is straightforward and clear, leaving no room for shame or misinterpretation. For example:

- A bad apology may sound like: "I'm sorry you got hurt by my actions."
- A good apology may sound like: "I'm sorry I hurt you."

Sincere apologies always focus on our genuine acknowledgment of how we contributed to the unpleasantness of the situation. Even if we did little wrong, we may even offer an apology for the sake of repair. For example:

- "I'm so sorry for arguing with you."
- "I can see now how much you're hurting. I'm so sorry."
- "I'm sorry I didn't understand your side of things sooner."

Taking the time to actively state our sincere apologies during the repair process is incredibly powerful and can go a long way. It may even harbor enough trust and emotional repair to drastically speed up our reconnection and healing.

E - Empathize With Our Partners Through Active Support

Once we've reached a point of open communication, acknowledged each other's emotions, and apologized, we need to end the repair process with a long-term commitment to active support. We need to continue empathizing with our partners and showing up for them throughout the healing process.

If both partners comfortably support each other while repairing the connection, both partners will receive adequate support to keep moving forward. It can be difficult to empathize with our partners when we're hurt, especially if they've done something to damage the connection. However, if we hope to repair the relationship, empathy is a necessity. We must remain a team and continue to care about each other's experience.

Seeking Professional Support When Needed

Occasionally, ruptures of trust or breakdowns in our relationships may require professional support. A great relationship can endure much turmoil with the right knowledge and assistance. Knowing when to seek help and acknowledging therapy as a useful and viable tool for our relationships can significantly enhance them.[92] We can receive feedback tailored to our specific relationship dynamics and feel supported to make it through tough spots more successfully. We may need to seek professional support when our relationships experience:[93]

- Persistent conflict that includes recurring themes, unresolved issues, and ongoing tension.

- Emotional distance in one or both partners that may include a lack of intimacy, isolation, or feelings of disconnection.

- Broken trust accompanied by unshakable suspicion, jealousy, and difficulties rebuilding trust on our own.

- Major life transitions that impact the relationship in unforeseen ways, such as illness, financial strain, or moving to a new state or country.

- Attachment behaviors that are not being addressed or seeing improvements with consistent effort.

Even if we put a lot of work into our personal growth and the development of our relationships, we may have blind spots regarding certain issues. Working with an experienced therapist can help us address any blind spots and make progress on challenges specific to our relationships.

Cultivating secure behaviors can significantly improve your relationships. However, relationships take two to be fulfilling. Who you choose to be in relationships with is just as important as your ongoing self-development.

CREATING SECURE ATTACHMENT IN FUTURE RELATIONSHIPS

Recognizing secure attachment in others can save us a lot of pain. When we surround ourselves with secure people, we can experience the level of safety needed in relationships to heal our attachment wounds.[94] If we can trust the people we're around to have good intentions and a healthy relationship ethic, then we can better guage how much of our anxiety is true and how much is anxious attachment.

The list of secure behaviors is a great start in understanding what secure attachment entails. However, reflecting on how it feels to connect with securely attached people may serve us better in this scenario. In your Workbook, reflect on any interactions or relationships you've had with people that seemed secure. It's important that we learn how to spot secure attachment and surround ourselves with people who are emotionally available to naturally negate anxious flare-ups and give ourselves space to heal. Relationships with secure people may involve:

- Consistent feelings of safety.
- Predictable and fair reactions to conflict.
- Kind words and affirming language.
- Genuine support and encouragement.
- Empathy and understanding.
- Respect for needs and boundaries.
- Balanced independence and autonomy.
- Consistent emotional availability.
- Joy, playfulness, and contentment.

Being with secure people will likely feel less triggering, more comfortable, and straightforward. There shouldn't be any confusion about how they feel about us or what their intentions are. Provided we are working to heal and show up securely, being around secure people should ease our anxiety in many ways and provide a model for healthy relationships we can aspire to.

With these healthy relationship aspects in mind, we can move forward with clear boundaries of what we expect from relationships. We can be sure to accept nothing less than fair, honest, and reliable treatment. While relationships are a great place to grow and learn about ourselves, they shouldn't be causing us significant stress or anxiety.

If our current relationships trigger anxious behaviors or cause us stress, we don't necessarily have to discard them. However, if we want to experience the peace and fulfilling love that genuine, secure connections can bring, we have to be willing to enforce clear boundaries for our partners to meet. We can give them opportunities to grow with us and make the consequences of staying the same clear.

Enforcing boundaries may initially create conflict or end challenging relationships. But it's important that we continue to grow and strive for the relationships we deserve despite any initial setbacks. We need to trust in our journeys and aim to attract healthy love.

CONCLUSION: EMBRACING THE ONGOING JOURNEY OF GROWTH AND CONNECTION

Fostering secure attachment is an ongoing journey that may involve many setbacks. As we continue to face our fears and expand our comfort zones, old patterns, and wounds may surface from time to time. With time and a commitment to embracing the skills, insights, and self-awareness we have developed since Chapter 1, healing is a natural consequence.

Healthy love must remain our top priority if we are to experience full transformation and ease in relationships. We must ensure our well-being, boundaries, and energy are preserved so that we can show up as the secure people we want to be—no longer plagued by The Self-Sabotage Cycle Of Anxious Attachment.

When you're ready, please turn the page for some final reflections and regards. There's one last thing I'd like to reflect on with you before you finish this book and take what you've learned into your world.

IN 90 SECONDS YOU CAN MAKE A HUGE DIFFERENCE

If you feel we've deserved it, please take a moment to leave a review on Amazon.

Your feedback means the world to us. It helps us to improve and it means better learning experiences for all our readers.

We'd be so grateful to you for your review!

Thank you!
Thank you!
Thank you!

CONCLUSION

EMBRACING YOUR JOURNEY AND MAINTAINING PROGRESS

Seeing you here at the end of the book is an incredible testament to your commitment to creating love. I'm proud of you, and I'm grateful to be part of this journey with you.

While you may be at the end of the book, this is far from the end of the journey. Arguably, the beginning. Secure love isn't something that lasts while it feels good or while you're not facing challenges. It's you, from from now on. Thick and thin, through everything. It's your new approach.

However, beware, the cycle of self-sabotage looms everpresent. The temptation to shrink, to slide into old habits, and to blame your partner for how you feel will always pose a threat, but your resistance is made in the habits you form. If you choose to use the tools I've shared with you in the way I've suggested, your resistance will be impenetrable. However, if you wait until problems emerge before you take steps to build trust, create intimacy, take a deep breath, regulate your emotions, or any of the other sensible things you know how to do, you could succumb to the same anxious thoughts that led you here in the first place.

The great news is, the way to resist the draw of the Self-Sabotage Cycle is to simply take one step in the opposite direction, stay on that path and the rest will follow.

Here's your arsenal. Use them. They work:

- **The Toolkit:** Including The EGO Technique, The ERS Technique, and The Calm Coping Technique for short and long-term management of our behaviors, thoughts, and emotions.

- **Self-Confidence:** Building a strong sense of self so you can show up in relationships more authentically.

- **A Secure Communication Style:** Asserting your needs and boundaries while maintaining empathy.

- **Trust, Vulnerability, And Intimacy:** Effective ways to deepen connections and feel more secure in your relationships.

- **The CARE Repair Technique:** Your ultimate conflict resolution strategy for building and repairing secure relationships.

With these, and your commitment, you have what it takes to create a love that is beautiful and whole. Don't doubt yourself. Anxious attachment doesn't have to be in control anymore. Take these skills and continue to apply them through every setback, argument, or relationship break down. I promise, with time and consistency, you will see positive change as I did. My most profound change came when I was at my lowest. Plus, you're not alone. Support is abundant in the LearnWell Community.

Just keep going.

With secure and lasting love,
Greta 🖤

REFERENCES

1. Paula Dagnino, et al., 2007, Depression and Attachment: How do Personality Styles and Social Support Influence This Relation?, Retrieved from:https://www.researchinpsychotherapy.org/rpsy/article/view/237/212

2. Itziar Alonso Arbiol, et al., 2002, Insecure Attachment, Gender Roles, And Interpersonal Dependency In Basque Country, Retrieved from:https://adultattachment.faculty.ucdavis.edu/wp-content/uploads/sites/66/2015/09/Alonso-Arbiol_2002_Insecure-attachment-gender-roles-and-interpersonal-dependency.pdf

3. Eric Patterson, LPC, 2022, Hypervigilance: Signs, Symptoms & Treatments, Retrieved from:https://www.choosingtherapy.com/hypervigilance/

4. Zeynep Set, et al., 2019, Potential Regulatory Elements Between Attachment Styles and Psychopathology: Rejection Sensitivity and Self-esteem, Retrieved from:https://www.ncbi.nlm.nih.gov/pmc/articles/PMC6732807/

5. Hal Shorey Ph.D., 2022, Attachment, Jealousy, and Excessive Reassurance Seeking, Retrieved from:https://www.psychologytoday.com/za/blog/the-freedom-change/202207/attachment-jealousy-and-excessive-reassurance-seeking

6. Rebecca Joy Stanborough and Debra Rose Wilson Ph.D.,2022, What Are Cognitive Distortions and How Can You Change These Thinking Patterns?, Retrieved from:https://www.healthline.com/health/cognitive-distortions

7. Adabel Lee and Benjamin L. Hankin, 2009, Insecure Attachment, Dysfunctional Attitudes, and Low Self-Esteem Predicting Prospective Symptoms of Depression and Anxiety During Adolescence, Retrieved from:https://www.ncbi.nlm.nih.gov/pmc/articles/PMC2741157/

8. Irene Messina, et al., 2023, Attachment Orientations and Emotion Regulation: New Insights From the Study of Interpersonal Emotion Regulation Strategies, Retrieved from:https://www.ncbi.nlm.nih.gov/pmc/articles/PMC10849076/

9. Irene Messina, et al., 2023, Attachment Orientations and Emotion Regulation: New Insights From the Study of Interpersonal Emotion Regulation Strategies, Retrieved from:https://www.ncbi.nlm.nih.gov/pmc/articles/PMC10849076/

10. Hal Shorey Ph.D., 2023, How Protesting Ruins Relationships: Trying to elicit love with anger or threats never works., Retrieved from:https://www.psychologytoday.com/us/blog/the-freedom-to-change/202306/stop-the-relationship-protest

11. Stephanie A. Sarkis Ph.D., 2023, Why Anxious and Avoidant Attachment Attract Each Other, Retrieved from:https://www.psychologytoday.com/za/blog/here-there-and-everywhere/202306/why-anxious-and-avoidant-attachment-attract-each-other

12. Dore Lavering, 2014, The Relationships between Attachment Style and Boundary The Relationships between Attachment Style and Boundary Thickness, Retrieved from:https://aura.antioch.edu/cgi/viewcontent.cgi?article=1252&context=etds

13. Sandra Silva Casabianca and Saundra Montijo, 2022, Have an Unhealthy Attachment to Your Partner? Healing Is

References

Possible, Retrieved from:https://psychcentral.com/blog/healing-unhealthy-relationship-attachments

14. Sandra Silva Casabianca and Saundra Montijo, 2022, Have an Unhealthy Attachment to Your Partner? Healing Is Possible, Retrieved from:https://psychcentral.com/blog/healing-unhealthy-relationship-attachments

15. Nicole Busacker, 2022, Effects of Parents' Avoidant and Anxious Attachment on Children, Retrieved from:https://scholarsarchive.byu.edu/cgi/viewcontent.cgi?article=1093&context=familyperspectives

16. Neil Schneiderman,, et al., 2008, STRESS AND HEALTH: Psychological, Behavioral, and Biological Determinants, Retrieved from:https://www.ncbi.nlm.nih.gov/pmc/articles/PMC2568977/

17. National Institutes of Health, 2024, Understanding the Link Between Chronic Disease and Depression, Retrieved from:https://www.nimh.nih.gov/health/publications/chronic-illness-mental-health

18. Agnese Mariotti, 2015, The effects of chronic stress on health: new insights into the molecular mechanisms of brain–body communication, Retrieved from:https://www.ncbi.nlm.nih.gov/pmc/articles/PMC5137920/

19. Luc Staner, MD., 2003, Sleep and Anxiety Disorders, Retrieved from:https://www.ncbi.nlm.nih.gov/pmc/articles/PMC3181635/

20. Kaylee Dusang, 2019, How Stress Can Affect Your Sleep, Retrieved from:https://www.bcm.edu/news/how-stress-can-affect-your-sleep#:~:text=%E2%80%9CHigh%20levels%20of%20stress%20impair,disrupts%20sleep%2C%E2%80%9D%20Wilson%20explained

21. Eva Stormorken, et al., 2015, Fatigue In Adults With Post-Infectious Fatigue Syndrome: A Qualitative Content

Analysis, Retrieved from:https://www.ncbi.nlm.nih.gov/pmc/articles/PMC4662830/

22. William Shaw, PhD., et al., 2023, Stress Effects on the Body, Retrieved from:https://www.apa.org/topics/stress/body#:~:text=Muscle%20tension%20is%20almost%20a,less%20constant%20state%20of%20guardedness

23. Diane Benoit, MD, 2004, Infant-parent Attachment: Definition, Types, Antecedents, Measurement and Outcome, Retrieved from:https://www.ncbi.nlm.nih.gov/pmc/articles/PMC2724160/

24. Diane Benoit, MD, 2004, Infant-parent Attachment: Definition, Types, Antecedents, Measurement and Outcome, Retrieved from:https://www.ncbi.nlm.nih.gov/pmc/articles/PMC2724160/

25. Jannike Kaasbøll, et al., 2021, Parental Chronic Illness, Internalizing Problems in Young Adulthood and the Mediating Role of Adolescent Attachment to Parents: A Prospective Cohort Study, Retrieved from:https://www.ncbi.nlm.nih.gov/pmc/articles/PMC8758574/

26. Victoria State Government Department Of Health, 2012, Child Developmen: Six to Nine Months, Retrieved from:https://www.betterhealth.vic.gov.au/health/healthyliving/child-development-3-six-to-nine-months

27. Jacquelyn Cafasso and Timothy J. Legg, PhD, PsyD, 2019, What Is Anxious Attachment?, Retrieved from:https://www.healthline.com/health/mental-health/anxious-attachment

28. Nanu Elena Doinita and Nijloveanu Dorina Maria, 2015, Attachment and Parenting Styles, Retrieved from:https://www.sciencedirect.com/science/article/pii/S1877042815049307?ref=pdf_download&fr=RR-7&rr=8ab5408a39535d35

29. Zawn Villines and Kendra Kubala, PsyD., 2023, Can emotional abuse cause PTSD?, Retrieved from:https://

www.medicalnewstoday.com/articles/ptsd-from-emotional-abuse#:~:text=Some%20research%20suggests%20it%20may,chronically%20haunted%20by%20the%20abuse

30. Theresa Lahousen, et al., 2019, Psychobiology of Attachment and Trauma—Some General Remarks From a Clinical Perspective, Retrieved from:https://www.ncbi.nlm.nih.gov/pmc/articles/PMC6920243/#:~:text=On%20the%20other%20hand%2C%20exposure,distinct%20attachment%20patterns%20(7)

31. Michael D. De Bellis, MD, MPH and Abigail Zisk A.B., 2014, "The Biological Effects of Childhood Trauma", Retrieved from:https://www.ncbi.nlm.nih.gov/pmc/articles/PMC3968319/

32. David Susman, PhD and Kendra Cherry, MSEd, 2023, 4 Types of Attachment Styles, Retrieved from:https://www.verywellmind.com/attachment-styles-2795344#:~:text=Later%20Experiences%20Matter%2C%20Too&text=Those%20described%20as%20ambivalent%20or,a%20partial%20role%20in%20attachment

33. Toupey M. Luft, 2016, The Use of EMDR Therapy for Couples Considering Divorce: Theory and Practice, Retrieved from:https://cjc-rcc.ucalgary.ca/article/view/61070/pdf

34. Zilpah Sheikh, MD, 2024, Anxious Attachment: What It Is and How It Affects Relationships, Retrieved from:https://www.webmd.com/mental-health/what-is-anxious-attachment

35. Berit Brogaard D.M.Sci., Ph.D, 2015, How to Change Your Attachment Style, Retrieved from:https://www.psychologytoday.com/intl/blog/the-mysteries-love/201503/how-change-your-attachment-

style#:~:text=Someone%20who%20initially%20has%20a,early%20child%2Dcaregiver%20interactions%20can

36. Berit Brogaard D.M.Sci., Ph.D, 2015, How to Change Your Attachment Style, Retrieved from:https://www.psychologytoday.com/intl/blog/the-mysteries-love/201503/how-change-your-attachment-style#:~:text=Someone%20who%20initially%20has%20a,early%20child%2Dcaregiver%20interactions%20can

37. Cleveland Clinic, 2023, Attachment Styles, Retrieved from:https://my.clevelandclinic.org/health/articles/25170-attachment-styles

38. Cleveland Clinic, 2023, Attachment Styles, Retrieved from:https://my.clevelandclinic.org/health/articles/25170-attachment-styles

39. Carla Marie Manly, Ph.D., 2021, Which Attachment Styles Are Most Compatible In Relationships?, Retrieved from:https://www.mindbodygreen.com/articles/attachment-style-compatibility

40. National Collaborating Centre for Mental Health (UK), 2015, Children's Attachment: Attachment in Children and Young People Who Are Adopted from Care, in Care or at High Risk of Going into Care., Retrieved from:https://www.ncbi.nlm.nih.gov/books/NBK356196/

41. National Collaborating Centre for Mental Health (UK), 2015, Children's Attachment: Attachment in Children and Young People Who Are Adopted from Care, in Care or at High Risk of Going into Care., Retrieved from:https://www.ncbi.nlm.nih.gov/books/NBK356196/

42. National Collaborating Centre for Mental Health (UK), 2015, Children's Attachment: Attachment in Children and Young People Who Are Adopted from Care, in Care or at High Risk of Going into Care., Retrieved from:https://www.ncbi.nlm.nih.gov/books/NBK356196/

43. National Collaborating Centre for Mental Health (UK), 2015, Children's Attachment: Attachment in Children and Young People Who Are Adopted from Care, in Care or at High Risk of Going into Care., Retrieved from:https://www.ncbi.nlm.nih.gov/books/NBK356196/
44. National Collaborating Centre for Mental Health (UK), 2015, Children's Attachment: Attachment in Children and Young People Who Are Adopted from Care, in Care or at High Risk of Going into Care., Retrieved from:https://www.ncbi.nlm.nih.gov/books/NBK356196/
45. Michael G. Gottschalk, PhD and Katharina Domschke, MD, PhD, 2017, Genetics of Generalized Anxiety Disorder and Related Traits, Retrieved from:://www.ncbi.nlm.nih.gov/pmc/articles/PMC5573560/
46. Olivia Guy-Evans, MSc and Saul Mcleod, PhD, 2024, Anxious Attachment Style: Signs In Adults, How It Develops & How To Cope,, Retrieved from:https://www.simplypsychology.org/anxious-attachment-style.html
47. Olivia Guy-Evans, MSc and Saul Mcleod, PhD, 2024, Anxious Attachment Style: Signs In Adults, How It Develops & How To Cope,, Retrieved from:https://www.simplypsychology.org/anxious-attachment-style.html
48. Hilary I. Lebow and Jacquelyn Johnson, PsyD., 2022, Anxious Attachment Style: Signs, Causes, and How to Change, Retrieved from:https://psychcentral.com/health/anxious-attachment-style-signs#signs-of-anxious-attachment-style
49. Center for Substance Abuse Treatment (US), 2014, Trauma-Informed Care in Behavioral Health Services., Retrieved from:https://www.ncbi.nlm.nih.gov/books/NBK207191/
50. B A van der Kolk, 1994, The Body Keeps the Score: Memory and the Evolving Psychobiology of Posttraumatic Stress, Retrieved from:https://pubmed.ncbi.nlm.nih.gov/9384857/

51. Kirsten Nunez and Timothy J. Legg, PhD, PsyD, 2023, Fight, Flight, Freeze: What This Response Means, Retrieved from:https://www.healthline.com/health/mental-health/fight-flight-freeze
52. Katerina Rnic, et al., 2016, Cognitive Distortions, Humor Styles, and Depression, Retrieved from:https://www.ncbi.nlm.nih.gov/pmc/articles/PMC4991044/
53. John D. Kelly, IV, MD, 2019, Your Best Life: Managing Negative Thoughts—The Choice is Yours, Retrieved from:https://www.ncbi.nlm.nih.gov/pmc/articles/PMC6554130/
54. Peter Grinspoon, MD, 2022, How to Recognize and Tame Your Cognitive Distortions, Retrieved from:https://www.health.harvard.edu/blog/how-to-recognize-and-tame-your-cognitive-distortions-202205042738
55. Peter Grinspoon, MD, 2022, How to Recognize and Tame Your Cognitive Distortions, Retrieved from:https://www.health.harvard.edu/blog/how-to-recognize-and-tame-your-cognitive-distortions-202205042738
56. Raidah Bhuyan, et al., 2023, Loving Yourself – That's "Great Company!" Loving Yourself – That's "Great Company!", Retrieved from:https://scholar.valpo.edu/cgi/viewcontent.cgi?article=1446&context=jvbl
57. Kristin Neff, ND, The Three Components of Self-Compassion, Retrieved from:https://selfcompassion.web.unc.edu/what-is-self-compassion/the-three-components-of-self-compassion/
58. Akeem Marsh, MD and Amy Morin, LCSW, 2023, How Cognitive Reframing Works, Retrieved from:https://www.verywellmind.com/reframing-defined-2610419
59. Jack Bauer, et al., 2006, Insecure Narrative identity and eudaimonic well-being, Retrieved from:https://www.

researchgate.net/publication/23545619_Narrative_identity_and_eudaimonic_well-being

60. Christopher N. Cascio, et al., 2015, Self-Affirmation Activates Brain Systems Associated with Self-Related Processing and reward and is Reinforced by Future Orientation, Retrieved from:https://www.ncbi.nlm.nih.gov/pmc/articles/PMC4814782/

61. Emily Bucher, LISW, 2020, Why it's important to 'feel' all of your feelings, Retrieved from:https://wexnermedical.osu.edu/blog/why-its-important-to-feel-all-of-your-feelings

62. Mental Health America, ND, What is Emotional Intelligence and How Does it Apply to the Workplace?, Retrieved from:https://mhanational.org/what-emotional-intelligence-and-how-does-it-apply-workplace#:~:text=Emotional%20Intelligence%20(EI)%20is%20the,%2C%20empathy%2C%20and%20social%20skills

63. Kateri McRae and James J Gross, 2020, Emotion Regulation, Retrieved from:https://pubmed.ncbi.nlm.nih.gov/31961170/

64. Kirsten Weir, 2011, The Exercise Effect, Retrieved from:https://www.apa.org/monitor/2011/12/exercise

65. Jessica Stillman, 2022, The Best Way to End a Fight, According to Science: Take a Walk Together, Retrieved from:https://icccr.tc.columbia.edu/news-and-events/news/the-best-way-to-end-a-fight-according-to-science-take-a-walk-together/

66. Matthew W. Southward, et al., 2019, Emotions As Context: Do the Naturalistic Effects of Emotion Regulation Strategies Depend on the Regulated Emotion?, Retrieved from:https://www.ncbi.nlm.nih.gov/pmc/articles/PMC6693875/

67. Timothy J. Legg, PhD, PsyD and Lana Burgess, 2023, Eight Benefits of Crying: Why it's Good to Shed a Few Tears,

Retrieved from:https://www.medicalnewstoday.com/articles/319631#:~:text=Crying%20is%20a%20natural%20response,more%20than%20people%20may%20assume

68. Lora E. Park, et al., 2004, Attachment Styles and Contingencies of Self-Worth, Retrieved from:https://ubwp.buffalo.edu/selfandmotivationlab/wp-content/uploads/sites/91/2018/05/Park-Crocker-Mickelson-2004-PSPB.pdf

69. The University of Queensland Australia, ND, Self-Esteem and Self-Confidence, Retrieved from:https://my.uq.edu.au/information-and-services/student-support/health-and-wellbeing/self-help-resources/self-esteem-and-self-confidence

70. Laura Copley, Ph.D., 2024, Anxious Attachment Style: What It Is (+ Its Hidden Strengths), Retrieved from:https://positivepsychology.com/anxious-attachment-style/#how-anxious-attachments-can-be-a-strength

71. Brittany Nicole Collins, 2023, The Effects Of Secure, Ambivalent, And Avoidant Attachment Styles On Number Of Codependent Behaviors And Relationship Satisfaction, Retrieved from:https://digitalcommons.liberty.edu/cgi/viewcontent.cgi?article=5254&context=doctoral

72. Elly Belle and Timothy J. Legg, PhD, PsyD, 2020, The Effects of Emotional Neglect on Codependency, Retrieved from:https://www.healthline.com/health/mental-health/codependency-and-attachment-trauma#So-what-does-a-secure-attachment-style-end-up-looking-like

73. Noel Bell, MA, PG Dip Psych, UKCP, 2017, Know Your Attachment Style and Overcome Codependency, Retrieved from:https://www.counselling-directory.org.uk/memberarticles/know-your-attachment-style-and-overcome-codependency

74. Leon F Seltzer PhD, 2022, Dependence vs. Autonomy in Relationships: What's Ideal?, Retrieved from:https://www.

psychologytoday.com/us/blog/evolution-the-self/202205/dependence-versus-autonomy-in-relationships-what-s-ideal

75. Cecilia Effa and Akilah Reynolds, PhD, 2023, How Can You Fix an Anxious Attachment Style?, Retrieved from:https://medicalnewstoday.com/articles/how-to-fix-anxious-attachment-style

76. Francine Montemurro, ND, "I" Messages or "I" Statements, Retrieved from:https://www.bumc.bu.edu/facdev-medicine/files/2011/08/I-messages-handout.pdf

77. Sahar Andrade, MB.BCh, 2021, The Importance Of Setting Healthy Boundaries, Retrieved from:https://www.forbes.com/sites/forbescoachescouncil/2021/07/01/the-importance-of-setting-healthy-boundaries/

78. Chantelle Pattemore and Jennifer Litner, PhD, LMFT, CST, 2023, How to Set Boundaries in Your Relationships, Retrieved from:https://psychcentral.com/relationships/why-healthy-relationships-always-have-boundaries#ineffective-boundaries

79. Jo Nash, Ph.D. , 2018, How to Set Healthy Boundaries & Build Positive Relationships, Retrieved from:https://positivepsychology.com/great-self-care-setting-healthy-boundaries/#examples

80. Alisha Durosier, 2024, How to Set Healthy Boundaries in School, Work, Life, and Relationships, Retrieved from:https://admissions.usf.edu/blog/how-to-set-healthy-boundaries-in-school-work-life-and-relationships

81. Chantelle Pattemore and Jennifer Litner, PhD, LMFT, CST, 2023, How to Set Boundaries in Your Relationships, Retrieved from:https://psychcentral.com/relationships/why-healthy-relationships-always-have-boundaries#ineffective-boundaries

82. John Amodeo Ph.D., MFT, 2022, The Art of Moving From Conflict to Connection, Retrieved from:https://www.psychologytoday.com/za/blog/intimacy-path-toward-spirituality/202206/the-art-moving-conflict-connection
83. Lindsey M. Rodriguez, PhD, et al., 2015, The Price of Distrust: Trust, Anxious Attachment, Jealousy, and Partner Abuse, Retrieved from: https://www.ncbi.nlm.nih.gov/pmc/articles/PMC5380380/
84. Lindsey M. Rodriguez, PhD, et al., 2015, The Price of Distrust: Trust, Anxious Attachment, Jealousy, and Partner Abuse, Retrieved from: https://www.ncbi.nlm.nih.gov/pmc/articles/PMC5380380/
85. Abigail P., 2024, Cultivating Trust: 8 Essential Components for Relationship Success, Retrieved from:https://extension.usu.edu/hru/blog/building-trust-in-relationships-guide-to-lasting-connection
86. Bethany Klynn, PhD, 2021, Building a Culture of Trust, Retrieved from:https://fisher.osu.edu/blogs/leadreadtoday/building-a-culture-trust
87. Abigail P., 2024, Cultivating Trust: 8 Essential Components for Relationship Success, Retrieved from:https://extension.usu.edu/hru/blog/building-trust-in-relationships-guide-to-lasting-connection
88. Audrey Brassard, et al., 2007, Attachment, Sexual Experience, and Sexual Pressure in Romantic Relationships: A Dyadic Approach, Retrieved from:https://adultattachment.faculty.ucdavis.edu/wp-content/uploads/sites/66/2015/09/Brassard_2007_Attachment-sexual-experience-and-sexual-pressure.pdf
89. Michael Crowe, 2018, Couple Relationship Problems and Sexual Dysfunctions: Therapeutic Guidelines, Retrieved from:https://www.cambridge.org/core/journals/advances-in-psychiatric-treatment/

article/couple-relationship-problems-and-sexual-dysfunctions-therapeutic-guidelines/A9BE6BC2E5E4108576DEF184A3CD762B?utm_campaign=shareaholic&utm_medium=copy_link&utm_source=bookmark

90. Audrey Brassard, et al., 2007, Attachment, Sexual Experience, and Sexual Pressure in Romantic Relationships: A Dyadic Approach, Retrieved from:https://adultattachment.faculty.ucdavis.edu/wp-content/uploads/sites/66/2015/09/Brassard_2007_Attachment-sexual-experience-and-sexual-pressure.pdf

91. Scott Frothingham and Timothy J. Legg, PhD, PsyD, 2019, What Is Secure Attachment and How Do You Develop One with Your Child?, Retrieved from:https://www.healthline.com/health/secure-attachment-2#secure-attachment

92. Sara Lindberg and Alex Klein, PsyD, 2020, Benefits and Options for Therapy, Retrieved from:https://www.healthline.com/health/benefits-of-therapy#couples

93. Razia Jeane, 2023, When to Seek Professional Help for Your Relationship, Retrieved from:https://extension.usu.edu/strongermarriage/blog/professional_help_relationships

94. Cecilia Effa and Akilah Reynolds, PhD, 2023, How Can You Fix an Anxious Attachment Style?, Retrieved from:https://www.medicalnewstoday.com/articles/how-to-fix-anxious-attachment-style#step-2-learning-from-others

www.ingramcontent.com/pod-product-compliance
Lightning Source LLC
Chambersburg PA
CBHW020413080526
44584CB00014B/1302